FLYING SOLO

HOW TO START AN INDIVIDUAL PRACTITIONER CONSULTING BUSINESS

Stuart G. Walesh PhD, PE
Consultant

Hannah Publishing
Valparaiso, IN 46385

Library of Congress Catalog Card Number :00-92065

ISBN 0-9701438-0-X

First Printing, July 2000
10 9 8 7 6 5 4 3 2 1

Additional copies of this book are available by mail.
Send $39.95 (includes tax and postage) to:

Hannah Publishing
3006 Towne Commons Drive
Valparaiso, IN 46385-2979
HannahPublishing@aol.com

Printed in the U.S.A. by
Morris Publishing
3212 East Highway 30
Kearney, NE 68847
1-800-650-7888

To Jerrie

Stuart G. Walesh

Dr. Stuart G. Walesh, PE is a sole proprietor management, marketing, training and education consultant to engineering firms and other private and public technical organizations. He has over 30 years of engineering and management experience in the government and private sectors. During that time, he has used and provided consulting services. Walesh has functioned as a project manager, department head, discipline manager, marketer, professor, and dean of an engineering college. He served as a project manager on many and varied projects ranging from small, focused studies to large, interdisciplinary, multi-office, multi-organizational efforts.

Recent projects for public and private sector clients include assisting clients in areas such as mentoring, coaching, marketing plans, proposal preparation, project management, re-engineering, education and training, creating a corporate university, facilitating national meetings, resolving personnel problems, technical writing, and career development. Clients served include the American Society of Civil Engineers, Bonar Group, Camp Dresser & McKee, Donohue & Associates, Earth Tech, PBS&J, Rust Environment and Infrastructure, University of Nebraska, U.S. Environmental Protection Agency, Vanasse Hangen Brustlin, and the communities of Pendleton and Valparaiso, IN.

Besides writing three books, Walesh is author or co-author of over 100 publications and presentations in the areas of engineering and management practice and education. During the last two decades, he led or facilitated over 120 seminars, workshops and meetings throughout the U.S.

Tel: 219-464-1704
Fax: 219-464-2978
Email: stuwalesh@aol.com

Contents

Preface

PURPOSE

Flying Solo is designed primarily for engineers and other technical-scientific-computer professionals who, regardless of age, have knowledge and experience and the desire to be sole proprietor consultants. Sole proprietor, individual practitioner, and free lancer all mean the same thing. They mean ownership of a business by one person. As used in this book, these terms also mean one employee—you!

If you are "on the fence" regarding going out on your own, *Flying Solo* will help you make a "go" or "no go" decision. If it's a "go," this book will explain how to get started in a pragmatic, comprehensive manner. If you have recently gone into business for yourself, the ideas and information will be helpful in saving or accelerating your business.

BENEFITS

More specifically, *Flying Solo* offers you many benefits. This book will describe telltale signs that point to going out on your own, characterize the functions of consultants, explain success factors, assess your viability as a sole proprietor, and present the logistics of getting started. *Flying Solo* also outlines a simple but effective marketing strategy, suggests ways to be successful with a new client, offers project management ideas, lays out basic accounting steps, offers liability minimizing tactics, and addresses the possibility and consequences of failure. Overall *Flying Solo* will help you enjoy your work, increase your autonomy and income, and prepare you for a comfortable retirement.

ACKNOWLEDGEMENTS

Most of *Flying Solo* was written over a one and one-half year period during which I conducted a workshop and recorded an audio course on individual practitioner consulting, and read widely and thought deeply about being a successful sole proprietor. The book draws on my years of experience, first part-time and then full-time, as a free lance consultant. Hopefully, *Flying Solo* also reflects my enthusiastic appreciation for the many benefits of being a sole proprietor consultant including autonomy, continuous learning, variety, good earnings, and the opportunity to help individuals and organizations create their futures.

I clearly recognize and sincerely appreciate ideas, information, and materials provided by others. The many and varied contributions of clients, workshop participants, other consultants, and colleagues are recognized, to the extent feasible, by citing them in the text and listing them in the References section. In particular, I appreciate Jeff Russell's suggestions which resulted in adding the negotiation discussion appearing in Chapter 4. John Hardwick and John MacDonald provided the concept for and some of the content of Chapter 12.

Book writing labor and logistics are challenging. I gratefully acknowledge the accurate, prompt, and creative word processing and graphics work of sole proprietor, Vicki L. Farabaugh, owner of Creative Computing. Sylvia S. Cutler, Editorial Consultant, added value by her thorough editing and many helpful suggestions. Jerrie, my wife, provided source materials, constructively critiqued the entire text, and as always, provided total support.

Stuart G. Walesh
Cape Haze, Florida
July 2000

List of Abbreviations

A	assets
ACEC	American Consulting Engineers Council
A/E	architect/engineer
ASCE	American Society of Civil Engineers
AV	audiovisual
CADD	computer aided drafting and design
CEO	chief executive officer
COBRA	Consolidated Omnibus Reconciliation Act (of 1985)
CPA	Certified Public Accountant
CU	corporate university
E	equity (same as NW) or expense
E&T	education and training
FAA	Federal Aviation Administration
FEMA	Federal Emergency Management Agency
GIS	geographic information system
GUTS	give up too soon
I	income

IRS	Internal Revenue Service
KISS	Keep it simple, stupid
L	liabilities
M	multiplier
NASE	National Association for the Self-Employed
NI	Net income
NPDES	National Pollution Discharge Elimination System
NSPE	National Society of Professional Engineers
NW	net worth (same as E)
PM	project management
R&D	research and development
RFP	request for proposal
SBA	Small Business Administration
SBDC	Small Business Development Center
SEP	Simplified Employee Program
SOHO	Small office, home office
SOQ	statement of qualifications
TQM	total quality management
USEPA	U.S. Environmental Protection Agency
WBT	web-based training

Chapter 1

Introduction

He who walks in another's tracks leaves no footprints. (Joan L. Brannon)

SOME QUESTIONS FOR YOU

Is your job security fading? Is the corporate bureaucracy getting you down? Are you increasingly concerned about how much you work and how little you earn? How about how hard you work and how little you learn? Are you tired of talk about pay for performance? Are you stagnating intellectually and/or emotionally? Do you want autonomy? Are challenges few and far between? Do you increasingly think, "I could do it better?" Are you retired but still "have the itch?"

Then ***maybe now is the time to "fly solo," to go out on your own—to start a sole proprietor, individual practitioner, or free lance consulting business*** that builds on your experience and vision. Remember, you only get to go around once.

Sole proprietor, individual practitioner, and free lance all mean the same thing. They mean ownership of a business by one person. As used in this book, these terms also ***mean only one employee—you!*** According to Boldt (1993, p. 351), "the term free lance has come down to us from medieval times when knights, independent of any lord, roamed the countryside in search of adventure. Because they were unattached, they were known as free lances." Boldt (1999, p. 352) notes that "a free lance is not interested in starting an organization," at least not in the traditional sense. Perhaps you've had enough of organizations. A free lance works at times when he or she feels most creative and has the most energy.

PURPOSE OF THIS BOOK

For engineers and other technical professionals who are "on the fence," the purpose of this book is to ***help make a "go" or "no go" decision*** regarding flying solo and, if it's a "go," to ***describe how to get started***. Book content is practical and immediately applicable.

If someone has recently gone into business for himself or herself, the practical and comprehensive ideas and information in this book will be helpful in saving or accelerating your new business. Topics include reasons to consider going out on your own, the roles of consultants, consulting success factors, assessing personal strengths and weaknesses, keeping current, logistics of office location and equipment, marketing, being successful with your first client, project management, business and personal accounting, profit drivers, liability minimization, consequences of failure, and special resources.

EXPECTED BENEFITS

As a result of reading this book, you should be able to:

- Recognize telltale signs that point to going out on your own.

- Understand the range of possible functions of consultants.
- Recognize the price of success.
- Assess your viability as a sole practitioner (do you have what it takes?).
- Maintain currency of skills and knowledge.
- Make a "go" or "no go" decision.
- Set up your office and legal form of organization.
- Develop a positive, simple approach to marketing.
- Set fees and keep financial score.
- Review project management principles.
- Minimize liability.
- Face the possibility of failure and what to do about it.
- Increase autonomy and income.
- Prepare for a comfortable retirement.

FRAME THE BIG PICTURE

Before you make a life-changing decision, give yourself enough time to think through the entire process. Introspection now will help you to avoid regrets later. This book will help you work through the evolutionary process, and by the time you have finished, you will know what you want to do, and be able to do it.

Starting a sole proprietorship will require a major personal effort. It could, if you are not careful, consume you. In your zeal for success, you might neglect your family, friends, and community and later have great regrets. Therefore, now might be an appropriate time to take stock of your overall situation. Establish or confirm your overall framework. Reflect on your roles and goals.

Roles—Then Goals

In the first part of the new year, many of us make—and soon often break—annual resolutions or goals. Our good intentions don't pan out. Goals deemed worthy on January 1 no longer seem to warrant special efforts. What's wrong? One answer may be that our resolutions and goals have no context. Our frustrating failure frequently follows from lack of relevance of the resolutions and goals to our overall life. Our resolutions and goals may be too narrowly focused, such as on our job, to the exclusion of our other areas of responsibility and opportunity.

One way to enhance the relevance of our goals is to cast them in terms of our desired roles. Adopt a holistic approach. That is, we should first select our key roles in life, at least for the foreseeable future. Then make resolutions or establish goals that will help us fulfill those valued roles. (This role-goal idea comes from the Covey Leadership Center). Mahatma Gandhi pointed to the need to identify our key roles and act on them when he said:

> *One man cannot do right in one department of life whilst he is occupied doing wrong in other departments. Life is one indivisible whole.*

An example of a non-work role that is likely to be shared by a potential free lancer is parent. Other common non-work roles are daughter, son, wife, husband, neighbor, church or synagogue member, athlete, and friend. As noted in the preceding sentence, "common" means a role likely to be held by many individuals, as opposed to a rare role. "Common" does not mean unimportant. Examples of work-related roles likely to be held by a potential sole proprietor are designer, administrator, marketer, project manager, partner, mentor, committee member, and officer in a professional, business, or service organization.

Although many of us share some roles, our interpretations of success in any given role will vary widely. Consider, for example, the non-work role of a neighbor. Some of us probably think that we successfully fulfill our neighborly responsibilities by quietly going about our business. Others would say that success in the neighbor role requires proactive involvement with many area residents.

Clearly, we can establish goals without first defining roles. The danger is that we will inadvertently omit or diminish important segments of our being. We risk incurring deep regrets that cannot be remedied. In contrast, the suggested "roles—then goals" process has the advantage of causing each of us to strive for balance in our life. That balance is especially important for the sole proprietor.

Smart Goals

Clear goals are crucial to charting and navigating the tumultuous seas of our professional, community and personal life. As stated in the Koran:

> *If you don't know where you are going, any road will get you there.*

As a guide to formulating annual or other goals, consider using the acronym ***SMART***.

- ***S*** means be ***S***pecific. A vague goal, such as "become a better member of the community" isn't very helpful. Instead try to be more specific such as "become an active member of a Chamber of Commerce committee."

- ***M*** stands for ***M***easurable in that, to the extent feasible, each goal should be cast in quantitative terms. An example is "obtain two new clients in the next calendar year." That which is measurable is more likely to get done.

- ***A*** refers to ***A***chievable. While we should be stretched by goals, we must be able to accomplish each one assuming a sustained, good-faith effort. A major goal, such as publishing a book, could be broken into ambitious subgoals, the first of which might be "sign a contract with a publisher."

- ***R*** denotes ***R***elevant in that each goal must be relevant to your chosen roles and other constraints. Establishing a goal of starting a service or project line in your individual practitioner business that is at odds with your strategic and business plans fails the relevance test.

- ***T*** represents ***T***ime-framed. Establish a schedule or milestones for achieving a goal or its components.

We are most likely to fulfill our chosen roles if we are guided by well formulated goals. Are your goals ***SMART***, that is, specific, measurable, achievable, relevant and time-framed?

WORKSHOP

A one day workshop, using *Flying Solo* as the principal resource, is available. Individuals or groups interested in partnering in offering *Flying Solo*, or a related workshop, should contact the author.

REVIEW

In summary, the "Introduction" of this book poses questions the answers of which could point you towards seriously exploring a sole proprietor, individual practitioner or free lance consulting business. The purpose of this book is to help you make a "go" or "no go" decision about going on your own and, if it's a "go," to describe how to get started. Creating a successful sole proprietorship requires a major, sustained effort. Don't let it consume you. Suggestion: Before making "a go" decision, frame the big picture. Consider family, friends, and community. Define desired roles and then set appropriate ***SMART*** goals.

A final thought, offered by Mark Twain:

> *Keep away from people who try to belittle your ambitions. Small people always do that, but the really great make you feel that you, too, can become great.*

Chapter 2

Telltale Signs: Some Reasons to Consider "Going Out on Your Own"

The greatest of all human benefits, that, at least, without which no other benefit can be truly enjoyed, is independence. (Parke Goodwin)

REASONS FOR FLYING SOLO

Ask a dozen entrepreneurs why they "went out on their own" and you are likely to get many and varied explanations. Experience suggests that some of the reasons will be more common. Seven of the more common motivators are explored in this chapter. They are shown in FIGURE 2-1 and discussed in following sections. You may find yourself in one or more of the seven categories and, as a result, gain additional insight into your situation. Perhaps your options will become more evident.

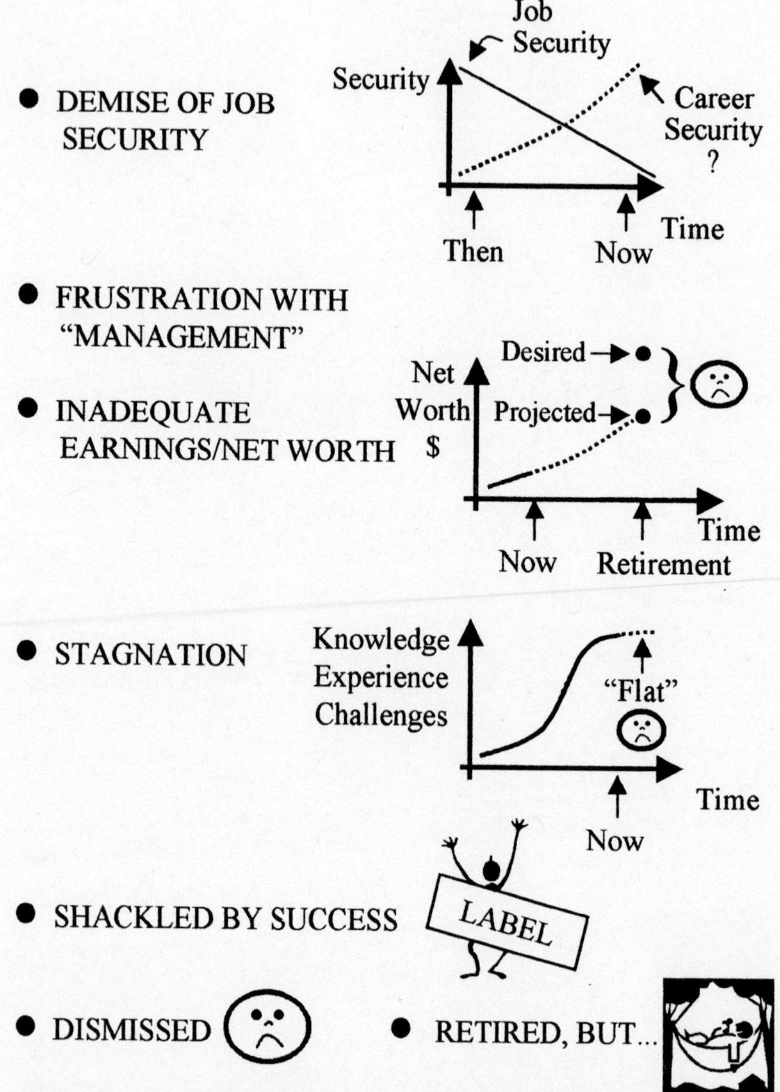

Figure 2-1. Any one of these seven signs could point to going out on your own.

DEMISE OF JOB SECURITY

Job Security: The Way It Used To Be

About 30 years ago, the author called his mother to tell her he was leaving his first real job. She was dismayed even though he was leaving by his choice. His mother lived through the hard times of the Great Depression when, if you were lucky enough to have a job, you did everything you could to keep it. Mother knew the importance of a secure job. A decade after the Depression, the U.S. was in World War II, and a decade later our country was the global economic leader. Workers and employers entered into informal agreements whereby workers gave a day's work for a day's pay and the employer provided a secure job. Workers received gold watches after 25 years of service. ***Job security was a fact***.

Job Security Dies

Gold watches and job security are things of the past. In January, 1996, AT&T announced a three-year workforce reduction. The company would cut its payroll by 50,000 employees. Most cuts would be in "white-collar" positions, including many engineering positions. As a reason for the cuts, the company cited increased competition that had led to ***increased productivity*** and the need for less personnel.

Personal productivity has increased partly because of computers and other technical tools. However, the amount of work expected of employees, including engineers, has increased at an even greater rate. Most people, including engineers, ***work longer and harder*** than they ever have. Bottom line: employers don't need as many personnel as they used to.

The rise of ***competent foreign competition*** and the development of a global economy threaten traditional U.S. technical professionals. Consider California's Silicon Valley, the world's largest producer of computer software. As explained in a *Chicago Tribune* article (Sept. 9, 1994), Bangalore, India, is the second-largest software producer, and Indian software engineers earn one-tenth the pay of Silicon Valley engineers. Today, software can be written anywhere and can be transmitted electronically. Is there any reason to suppose that U.S. engineering firms won't, using electronic tools, increasingly subcontract work to lower-paid engineers in other countries?

Outsourcing and the use of subconsultants and temporary contract employees started in janitorial services and back-office work such as payroll services. Now, it is rapidly moving into high-level, white-collar positions. According to the Economic Policy Institute, self-employed individuals make up 20% of the U.S. workforce.

Engineers working on a ***contingent basis*** (sole proprietors or contract professionals placed through an agency or "job shop," as they are often called) appear to be on the rise. Contingent workers offer many benefits to employers such as greater ability to accommodate rise and fall of work volume, improved access to needed specialties, reduced recruitment and other costs, and fewer personnel problems. Benefits cited for contingent workers include much less need to play office politics, greater diversity of assignments, more travel opportunities, avoiding being "promoted" into less satisfying management positions, and more control over schedule (Davis, 2000).

Ten years ago, private sector engineering executives often boasted about growth in the number of employees in their organizations. Today, they are much more likely to ***boast about employee reduction*** and higher profits. Engineers in public service are threatened by the ***re-engineering*** movement and various forms of ***privatization***. The private sector has demonstrated that it can often operate what have traditionally been publicly owned and operated facilities with less personnel.

Finally, the ***acquisition and merger*** activity in the consulting engineering and construction businesses has taken its toll. Inevitably such transactions lead to major resignations and dismissals.

The Future: Career Security?

Job security is an oxymoron but career security doesn't have to be. One reason is the sole proprietor/individual practitioner/free lance option. Such a person can thrive in the changing world of work. The individual engineer practitioner serving several clients at any one time probably has more security than the full time employee of an engineering organization.

See Walesh (1997) for additional description of the loss of job security and what to do about it. The changing world of work is also discussed in the *Economist* (December 1999), by Nevins and Stumpf (1999) and by Walesh (1995, pp. 392-395).

FRUSTRATION WITH MANAGEMENT: I COULD DO IT BETTER

> *I must create a system or be enslaved by another man's.*
> (William Blake)

The "I could do it better" telltale sign that someone may be a candidate for flying solo can be "shaky" because it's usually based on ignorance. You've been watching the decision-making process in your organization and comparing it to your experiences and your management and leadership studies (you read widely and are taking management courses). The more you monitor the situation, the more you think you could do better. You are beginning to wonder what or if "they" are thinking.

Questionable administrative tasks, especially excessive reporting on what you are doing, is one bureaucratic frustration. Dickson (1978 p. 59) explains rampant reporting this way:

> *The more time you spend in reporting on what you are doing, the less time you have to do anything. Stability is achieved when you spend all of your time doing nothing but reporting on the nothing you are doing.*

Another symptom of bureaucratic excess, is being spread too thin. You are asked to do more and more—project management, marketing, hiring, retention, accounting, physical plant—with less and less. You begin to see, to borrow an expression from your college calculus course, where this is going in the limit. You will continue to do less and less on more and more until you are eventually doing absolutely nothing on everything! This is not the foundation on which accomplishment and satisfaction are built.

But how do you know that you could do better? Your management experience is limited to project management and department management. You have never managed or led an entire organization. That lack of experience, however, does not stop you from quietly visualizing yourself as the top decision-maker. Maybe the logical next step is to be a sole proprietor, a big fish in a small pond, rather than an increasingly frustrated employee, a small fish in a big pond. After all, you owe it to yourself to see if your "I could do it better" feelings are correct.

INADEQUATE EARNINGS AND NET WORTH

> *You can be young without money,*
> *but you can't be old without it.*
> (Tennessee Williams)

You started your career at an above average salary. And rightly so because you were an academic achiever and a leader in college as well as being a cooperative education student. You have continued your professional commitment and have become a widely recognized technical expert in your field.

But, you are beginning to worry that your earnings may be lagging. Partly as a result, your net worth (assets, such as value of home and retirement funds, minus liabilities such as mortgages and car loans) may be growing too slowly to assure you of a comfortable retirement. In fact, you recently projected the approximate net worth you will need for retirement. Your situation and assumptions were as follows:

Current age: 30
Current salary: $50,000/year
Assumed inflation: 3%/year
Desired retirement age: 62
Desired ratio of buying power at retirement to buying power today: 3
Expected earnings on net worth at retirement to provide income for retirement: 8%

Based on the given conditions, stated assumptions, and defined goals, your required net worth at age 62 is a whopping $4,800,000.00! You need to be a multi-millionaire! And you have only three decades to do it. Speaking of millionaires, Stanley and Danko (1996) in their book *The Millionaire Next*

Door, note that two-thirds of America's millionaires are self-employed.

You have meticulously tracked and projected your net worth. Even though you are prudent, you won't make the needed net worth unless you significantly increase your salary. And that doesn't seem too likely, given the history of your company. After all, "profits haven't been very good" and "we must plow money back into the company to remain competitive." You know about the income statements of consulting firms, although you haven't seen the statement for yours. As a result, you recognize that a firm could be making low or no profit and the principals are still taking out huge salaries. In fact, those high salaries may be the cause of the low or no profit.

There was some talk around the organization about "pay for performance," but nothing seems to be happening. Perhaps this is just another way in which you are being "dilbertized." For two reasons, you are not likely to enter the high salary and bonus-eligible ranks. First, there is a preponderance of "young" principals. Second, you've chosen a technical route and have been very successful. Unfortunately, marketers and managers tend to be more readily recognized and advanced in your firm.

Accordingly, you are looking at options that will, among other things, enable you to increase your income and more rapidly build your net worth. One possibility is moving to another engineering firm or a government agency. Another option is to free lance. After all, if you're going to work as hard as you do, you may as well work for yourself and, if successful, reap the monetary benefits.

STAGNATION

Stagnation means plateauing in terms of knowledge and skills. Another way to define stagnation is to say that an individual is stagnating when the desire for challenge is increasing while the feeling of autonomy (ability to act) to choose challenging assignments is declining. Stagnation can occur in both technical and non-technical areas.

You can determine if you are stagnating technically by asking questions like these:

- What leading edge computer programs have you learned how to use in the last year?
- What innovative technical approaches (problem diagnoses) and solutions (problem solving) did you initiate and/or lead in the last year?
- In what ways have your technical achievements been recognized by your peers and others in the past year? For example, have you received an award from a professional society, been given a high profile technical assignment within your organization, or become a member of a national technical committee?

If you give mostly "no's" to these kinds of questions, you are probably stagnating technically. Incidentally, the stagnation test has to do with improvement, not absolute levels. You may, for example, be using a very sophisticated computer model. However, you've been using it for years, know almost everything there is to know about it, have stopped learning about it and are getting bored. And, looking ahead, you will continue to work with this program. That's stagnation!

As already noted, you can also stagnate, that is, stop learning and growing in non-technical areas that may be valuable to you. For example, what have you learned in the past year about:

- Personal roles, goal setting and time management?
- Planning, conducting and following up on meetings?
- Project management?
- Marketing?
- Total quality management, re-engineering, corporate universities, design-build, privatization and other "hot" topics?

Maybe you need to explore options that will once again enable you to take on challenges, gain in knowledge and skills, and be more productive and happier in the process. Starting a sole proprietor consulting business may be the answer. It virtually guarantees being presented with challenges and gaining knowledge and skills.

SHACKLED BY SUCCESS: HINDERED BY HISTORY

Perhaps you've made significant, high profile contributions to your organization in a relatively narrow area. For example, you've worked hard to become a regionally or nationally recognized expert in the design of water treatment plants. You have designed large and small plants, plants treating surface water and ground water, and plants for public sector and private sector clients.

Frankly, you're tired of this and want to take on completely new challenges. More specifically, your goal is to move from the technical area to the non-technical area and become a marketer of sophisticated water supply services. You are confident of your ability to "re-invent" yourself. You've done it before. For example, early in your career you successfully conducted basic research at a university.

But, and this is the heart of your current situation, you are perceived by the principals of your firm as being able to successfully do only water treatment plant design. You've repeatedly told them about your marketing goal but this message just doesn't register with them. Ironically, you've done too good a job in water treatment plant design. You are labeled water treatment plant designer par excellence.

Lancaster (May, 1999) observes that the company may find that its best interests are served by keeping high tech personnel in high tech functions. After all, such specialists are difficult to replace. "Golden hand cuffs," such as higher salaries, bonuses, extra vacation days, prestigious titles, and other "perks" are used to lock in high tech personnel. This strategy may serve the organization but not the individual. If and when the shackled persons want to move into management, marketing or other non-technical functions, they will, according to Lancaster, face:

> *...the perception that they are nose-to-the-grindstone nerds lacking communication and leadership skills needed to become successful managers. To some extent, of course, the stereotype may be true.*

Accordingly, you may need to move on. One option is seeking employment with a competitor. But, knowing your work, they may also have you "pegged" or "labeled." Another option is to "go out on your own." That way, you can be, or at least try to be, what you want to be. Survival as an individual practitioner will require, among other things, that you be a proficient marketer.

DISMISSED

Being dismissed by your employer, especially unexpectedly, is truly a "sign" that one needs to explore options, unless, of course, you are independently wealthy. The dismissed person is likely to go through a series of strong, mostly negative feelings such as (some taken from Koltnow and Dumas, 1990, listed alphabetically so as not to imply any order): anger, anxiety, depression, despair, devaluation, failure, fear, inadequacy, jealousy, loss, mourning, sadness, self-doubt, shame, shock, and surprise.

Near the end of this process, most dismissed professionals will be exploring options. One of these is to become an individual practitioner. Maybe this disastrous dismissal can be turned into an overwhelming opportunity. Koltnow and Dumas (1990, p. 4) seem to think so when they say:

> *Getting fired gives you a long-overdue opportunity to reassess your likes and dislikes, reevaluate your priorities, and redirect your energies to achieve the position or career you really want. I'm not just talking about stopping to smell the roses here; I'm talking about planting a few new ones, too.*

A Rose by Any Other Name

Judging by the number and variety of words for it, being dismissed must be quite common. Consider this synonyms list (some of which come from Koltnow and Dumas, 1990): checkmated, dismissed, down-sized, fired, let go, pink-slipped, re-engineered, right-sized, terminated, transformed, and unemployed.

Speaking of numbers, Koltnow and Dumas (1990, p. 25) suggest that "not working up to par" is a minor reason for people being dismissed. It may account for only five to ten percent of all dismissals. Furthermore, and this is also according to Koltnow and Dumas (1990, p. 25), the "four main reasons" for firing are:

- ***New management:*** Consider the recent flood of acquisitions in the civil engineering field.
- ***Office politics:*** You leave a lot to be desired as a "schmoozer."
- ***Economics:*** The company needs to reduce labor costs and your time utilization has been a bit low the past few months.
- ***Personality conflicts:*** You and your new boss simply do not see eye to eye.

The point of all this: If you've been dismissed, or whatever euphemism you want to use, it's probably not your fault. Perhaps this thought will help you "get on with it." Even if the termination was largely your fault, that's history. Learn from the experience and move on. In the spirit of learning, consider interviewing your former, or soon to be, former boss (Lancaster, April, 1999).

Immediate Action Items

Flying solo is the focus of this book. Employed individuals usually have the luxury of considering this and other options at their leisure. In contrast, dismissed professionals need to quickly attend to certain matters before they pursue employment or sole proprietor options.

If you've been recently dismissed or may be dismissed (which could happen to any of us except sole proprietors!), the immediate action items listed below may interest you. These "first things first" suggestions are taken from Koltnow and Dumas (1990):

1. Determine if you are eligible for unemployment compensation (most people are) and, if so, register for it (p. 10).

2. Obtain a supply of personal business cards with your name, address, telephone, email, etc. and possibly a generic description of what you do or could do. Examples are: "Consultant," "Systems Analyst," and "Marketer" (pp. 11-13).

3. Decide on how you will accurately and favorably explain your dismissal to potential employers and/or clients. Try to work this out with someone in authority at your last place of employment so you know what they will say if asked. Examples of accurate and favorable explanations are:

    - "The company was going in a new direction and no longer needed my particular expertise" (p. 14).

    - "New management decided to bring in its own team" (p. 14).

4. Bring your resume up to date (pp. 16-17).

5. Consider continuing your health insurance. The Consolidated Omnibus Reconciliation Act of 1985 (COBRA) "...allows you the option of purchasing continued health insurance coverage after you've been terminated." This assumes, among other things,

that you were under a company insurance plan and "...not fired for gross misconduct" (p. 17).

6. "Don't sign anything until you've had time to think it through (or received professional advice)" (p. 246).

7. "Find out exactly what kind of severance package (if any) you're being offered." Ask about or negotiate for weeks/months of salary, out-placement services, secretarial/clerical assistance, use of an office, and reference letter(s) (p. 246).

Demoted or Bypassed

Being demoted is likely to be less traumatic than being dismissed; however, it can have serious consequences such as bruised ego and reduced income. Being passed over for the promotion you worked for, wanted, and expected can also be traumatic. While going out on your own might be the ultimate solution to demotion or being bypassed, some constructive short-term actions are needed.

Some of the ideas presented earlier for understanding dismissal are also applicable here. Stern (2000) offers specific suggestions for dealing with dismissal. They are also useful if you did not receive a sincerely expected promotion. All of these thoughts assume that you are continuing to work for your employer, at least for the time being. The suggestions are:

- "Don't be impulsive", that is, take a deep breath and think before speaking and acting.

- "Think positively", that is, demotion and missed promotions don't equate with incompetence. You can add value in many ways to your current employer or in other professional situations.

- "Don't react childishly", that is, avoid sulking, sabotage, and other immature behaviors likely to be destructive to you and your employer.
- "Deal honestly with colleagues", that is, talk to co-workers about your new or retained role.
- "Learn from the situation", that is, communicate frankly with the manager or managers who made the demotion or bypass decision.
- "Consider departing", that is, after you've done the preceding, apply the appropriate ideas and information presented in this book.

RETIRED, BUT STILL "HAVE THE ITCH"

So you have finally retired! The engineering or other technically oriented organization is no longer a major part of your life. In fact, it's history. You accomplished much and have many pleasant memories (and a few not so pleasant) but, frankly, you are happy to have most of it behind you. You are financially comfortable, perhaps have a second home, do some traveling, play golf and/or tennis, spend time with your children and grandchildren, are involved in the community, and have taken care of some loose ends.

But… there's some unfinished business and it has to do with business. You miss certain aspects of working. It's different strokes for different folks. For example, some miss technical challenges, some miss marketing, and for others its organizational issues. Furthermore, there are a few projects or functions that you had planned to work on or get into but somehow time ran out.

Pipher (1999, p. 256) in her book on society's elders, says:

> *We are socialized to believe that endless luxury and leisure are what will make us happy, but it is not true. Endless leisure leads to apathy and despair. What feels good to most people is being useful. What gives life meaning is its effects on other people. Rest feels good only if it is in contrast to work.*

The "work" referenced in the previous quote does not necessarily have to be paid work. It could be meaningful volunteer work. However, "being useful" may mean that you want to re-enter professional work as a paid free lancer.

Although retired, you still have depth and breadth of experience, a network of colleagues and former clients, an understanding of the market, and a basic ability with all of today's wonderful electronic communication tools. Perhaps you can re-enter the business and professional world largely on your own terms. Maybe you can work on what you want and when and where. Perhaps you should go out on your own as a sole proprietor consultant.

TAKE ONE MORE LOOK AT INTERNAL OPTIONS

Before voluntarily leaving your current employer, regardless of the reason, take one more look at internal options. This advice is especially important if you are employed in a large, complex and multi-office public or private organization. Some suggested reality checks, cast in the form of questions for you to answer, are:

- Do the appropriate decision-makers know of your professional desires and frustrations? Don't assume and don't rely on "osmosis." Certain individuals may know of one or more internal opportunities for you or even create them for you.

- Might an organizational change be imminent (e.g., acquisition, revamped structure, additional service lines, retirements, and new office) which would fit your need?
- Are your expectations realistic? While you shouldn't be guided by common or average thinking, you should determine if your expectations are within the realm of reality. Can you point to examples of others who have achieved what you want to achieve?

REVIEW

In summary, consider the key ideas in this chapter titled "Telltale Signs: Some Reasons to Consider Going Out on Your Own." Seven common reasons to seriously consider "going out on your own" are discussed. One or more is likely to apply to you. The seven motivators are:

1. ***Demise of job security*** and the possibility of career security as an alternative.
2. ***Frustration with management*** or "I could do it better."
3. ***Inadequate earnings and net worth***, particularly with an eye toward a comfortable retirement.
4. ***Stagnation***, that is, plateauing in terms of challenges, knowledge and skills.
5. ***Shackled by success***. The powers that be have narrowly labeled you based on your successes and cannot see you in the other roles you want to play.

6. ***Dismissed, demoted, bypassed.*** You are unemployed or soon will be. You've been demoted or passed over. All options are "on the table."

7. ***Retired***, but still "have the itch."

Before voluntarily leaving an employment situation, regardless of the motivation, take one more look at internal options before seeking employment elsewhere or becoming a free lance.

A closing thought, offered by Henry David Thoreau:

> *Go confidently in the direction of your dreams. Live the life you imagined.*

Chapter 3

Roles and Selection of Consultants

> *A consultant is someone hired to come a long distance to tell you the time of the day. The consultant borrows your watch, tells you the time, keeps your watch, and sends you a bill.* (Anonymous)

WHAT IS MEANT BY "CONSULTANT?"

Consider the typical owner-consultant-contractor interaction so common in civil engineering. As suggested by it, individuals and organizations requiring planning, design, management and other engineering-related services often retain consultants to provide those services. That is, rather than have the technical and/or non-technical work done "in-house," they choose to have it outsourced to a consultant.

What is meant by "consultant?" From a contractual, formal perspective, consultant usually means a ***consulting firm*** that enters into legal agreements with clients for the provision of services. However, on probing the matter further with owners and clients, "consultant" usually means a ***particular person***, or perhaps a small group of professionals, on the staff of a consulting firm who have demonstrated competence and established a high trust relationship with an individual or a small group on the staff of the client, customer or owner.

One indication of this second interpretation of "consultant" is the strong allegiance shown by those who use the services of consultants to individual technical professionals when the professionals change employers, that is, move from one consulting organization to another, or establish their own practice. This second interpretation of "consultant" suggests that a trustful relationship is critical in carrying out the consulting function—expertise is necessary, but clearly not sufficient. One of the highest compliments that an individual consultant can receive is to be retained on a sole-source basis by a client.

After exploring reasons why consultants are retained, this chapter describes the consultant selection process, which is sometimes extremely complex and costly. However, as a sole proprietor you may be able to avoid some of the complexity and costs.

WHY RETAIN A CONSULTANT?

Consultants, in the form of consulting firms or individual professionals, are typically retained for one or more of the following five reasons:

- **Temporarily acquire necessary expertise** – In this increasingly technological world, many public and private organizations, even those with engineers and other technical professionals on their staffs, do not have certain types of expertise. While they could develop such expertise, they are often reluctant to do so unless they see a continuous need for it. Accordingly, they seek a consultant having the necessary expertise for a temporary assignment. Prudent owners, desiring to develop in-house expertise, should consider contracting with one or more consultants to provide education and training (E&T) in the desired area of expertise in addition to completing the project at hand. Perhaps this E&T could be your service niche.

Incidentally, some of the needed expertise may be in non-technical areas. In fact, engineering firms, because of their technical focus, often turn to consultants, some of whom are individual practitioners, for non-technical services. Consultants who offer non-technical services while being knowledgeable about or coming from the engineering field have a special advantage. This is another possible niche for you.

- **Supplement in-house staff** – Regardless of whether or not an organization has the necessary engineering and other expertise in-house to carry out a project or accomplish a task, they may not have enough staff members available at a given time to complete the project or task on schedule. Accordingly, they solve their "people power" shortage through the temporary use of consultants. As a free lance, you may have the flexibility to immediately step in and be productive.

- **Provide absolute objectivity** – A public or private organization, even one that has wide and deep expertise and sufficient staff, may find itself embroiled in controversy, the resolution of which requires a high degree of objectivity. Perceived and perhaps actual objectivity are likely to be the greatest when an outside consultant is retained.

For example, a municipality may experience a heavy rainfall and resulting widespread flooding. This catastrophe may bring into question the adequacy of stormwater facilities designed by the municipality's professional staff or by consultants retained by the municipality. While the in-house professional staff or the consultant who did the original planning and design could certainly be asked to review the work, the most credible approach might be to retain an outside consultant to provide the highest level of objectivity. In this case, the preferred outside consultant would be an individual or organization that had the necessary technical and other expertise, had never provided services to the municipality before, and perhaps had its nearest office in another community or state. You might be that person.

- **Perform unpleasant tasks** – Carrying out unpleasant tasks or doing the "dirty work" is rarely the sole or principal purpose of a consultant, although it may be the principal purpose of a management consultant. However, engineering and other technical projects, particularly those in the public sector, often involve unpleasant and stressful tasks. For example, the long-term and frequent failure of crucial municipal facilities and services such as water supply, wastewater, transportation, and flood control can lead to deep-seated and widespread frustration among citizens of a community. Consultants are often retained to find a planning and engineering solution to such problems.

Regardless of the other reasons why consultants are retained, such as to provide expertise, needed staff, and objectivity, consultants are often also expected to release, deal directly with, and re-channel the pent-up frustration within the community. One effective mechanism is the conduct of neighborhood information meetings shortly after the consultant is retained. One or more representatives of the consulting organization are introduced and asked to provide an outlet for citizen frustration hopefully culminating in citizen confidence that the problems can and will be solved. One result could be a productive, on-going program of interaction between the professionals and the public (Walesh, 1993). Similar situations involving the need to provide an outlet for pent-up frustration and instill a spirit of cooperation and optimism also occur in the private sector. Consultants may also be asked to seek cooperation among private and public entities experiencing disagreement and conflict. Maybe you have a disposition and skill set that could help clients interact more effectively with their stakeholders.

- **Reduce liability** – This, the fifth and last reason presented here for retaining a consultant, should "raise a flag" for the individual practitioner. You may be retained partly or primarily to absorb risk that will be shifted from someone else or some other organization. Your client may be a consulting firm, a contractor, or a government entity.

Technical specialties within engineering that are generally considered to be more risky include geotechnical, structures, and hazardous waste. The sole proprietor offering these services should be especially cautious with contract/agreement language, exercise great care in performing tasks and writing reports, and secure errors and omissions insurance. Chapter 11 provides ideas on how to minimize your liability while serving the client.

In summary, consulting firms or individual consultants are typically retained for one or more of the following five reasons: to provide expertise, supplement in-house staff, offer a high degree of objectivity, perform unpleasant tasks, and reduce liability. Both parties, that is, the individual practitioner and the client, should strive to identify and prioritize the reason or reasons for needing the consultant prior to entering into a consultant-client agreement. Mutually satisfying outcomes depend on a clear understanding of needs and expectations.

Hopefully, as a result of the ideas and information presented here, you as the prospective free lance will view your role and responsibility as being more than simply doing assigned tasks and generating deliverables. At minimum, as you begin work on a new project, be sure you fully understand why the client retained you.

CONSULTANT SELECTION PROCESS

The process by which an owner selects a consultant to provide planning, design, construction, operations, management, training or other services is, at the detailed level, unique to each situation. However, much that is useful can be explained within the context of an overall approach or model as presented here. Similar and additional ideas and information on consultant selection are provided by Clough (1986, Chapter 4), Davis (1987), and Kasma (1987).

Cost Versus Quality

> *It is unwise to pay too much, but it is worse to pay too little. When you pay too much, you lose a little money, that is all. When you pay too little, you sometimes lose everything because the thing you bought is not capable of doing the thing it was bought to do. The common law of business balance prohibits paying a little and getting a lot--it can't be done. If you deal with the lowest bidder, you might as well add something for the risk you will run and if you do that, you will have enough to pay for something better.* (John Ruskin)

Very frequently, as illustrated in FIGURE 3-1, the consultant selection process is driven implicitly or explicitly by the natural tension that exists between the ***quality of service*** (conformance to requirements) that is likely to be received and the ***cost of service***. You routinely encounter the same tension in your personal life when you shop for clothing or select a restaurant for that special occasion.

In a very rough way, as proposed consulting fees for a given project diminish, the quality of the resulting plan, design, or other product is likely to diminish and the capital and other costs associated with the product are likely to increase. You get what you pay for.

Fees are certainly important. However, because fees can be readily quantified, relative to other selection factors such as

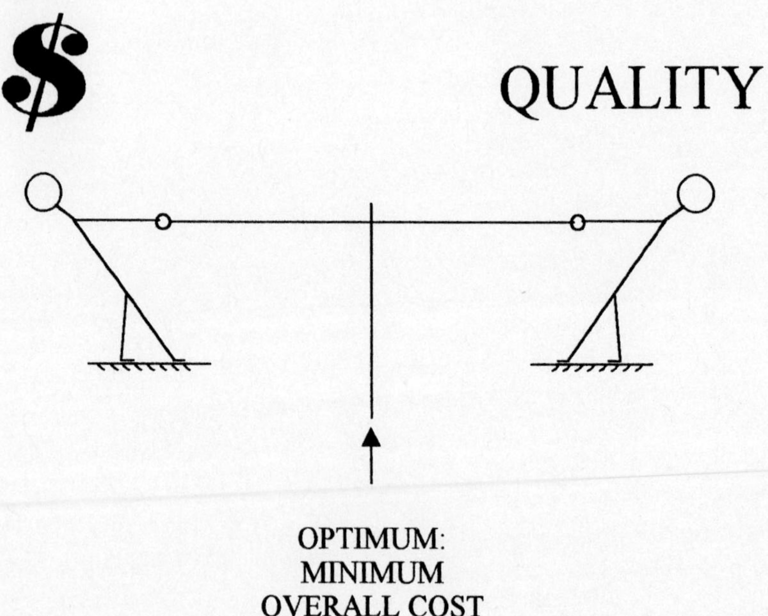

Note: Quality is defined as conformance to requirements.

Figure 3-1. The cost-quality tension is always present in the consultant selection process.

experience and creativity, they tend to assume excessive influence. As succinctly stated by Kasma (1987), "When price is a factor in selecting consultants for negotiations, it usually becomes the deciding factor, particularly in public organizations."

Unusually low fees proposed by consultants trying to obtain contracts sometimes reflect a lack of experience and, therefore, awareness of all necessary aspects of a project. At other times, low fees might reflect an individual consultant's or a consulting firm's desire to obtain a contract for a new type of project on which they can gain valuable experience. They are, in effect, willing to "buy" (lose money on) the assignment in exchange for the knowledge they will gain. As a new sole proprietor, you may decide to do this. If so, be aware of incurring excessive liability as discussed in Chapters 5 and 11 of this book.

Most people and organizations retaining consultants know that they should avoid being penny-wise and pound-foolish. However, a completely rational approach does not always prevail nor may it be possible because of insufficient information. Consultants must put themselves "in the shoes" of client's decision-makers, particularly those who are public officials subject to public scrutiny. They may be hard pressed to justify a larger proposed fee over a smaller proposed fee when, at least on the surface, the resulting proposed products appear identical. Remember, at the time of consultant selection, the total costs and benefits of the project are usually not known or are not perceived as an important factor.

Ideally, clients and owners should select consultants with the goal of minimizing their total costs, that is, the sum of the consulting fee, initial capital cost, and present the worth of operation and maintenance costs. This ideal selection concept is illustrated in FIGURE 3-2. The fees proposed by potential consultants A, B, and C vary widely with the largest fee being

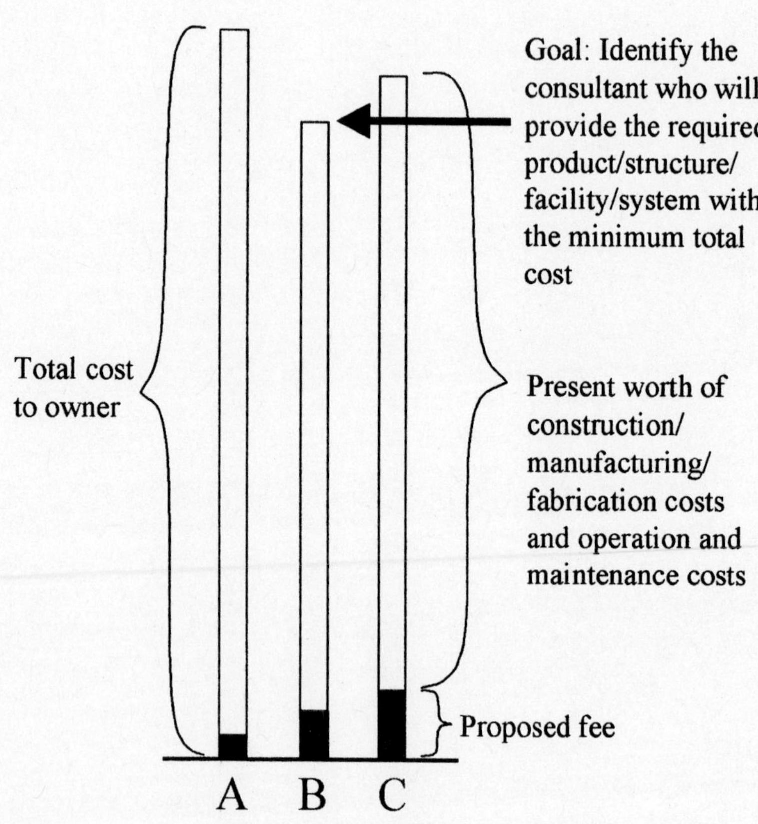

Figure 3-2. Ideally, consultant selection should consider total costs.

approximately twice the smallest fee. Similarly, there are significant variations, although not as dramatic in a relative sense, in the present worth of the construction/manufacturing/fabrication costs and operation and maintenance cost that would be incurred by the owner. Of course, as already noted, these total costs or even relative values of these costs are not likely to be known by the owner at the consultant selection stage. If they were known, or could be known, the owner would obviously determine the total cost associated with each of the three potential consultants and their likely products and select the consultant who would offer the lowest total cost. This would be consultant B in FIGURE 3-2.

Steps in the Selection Process

The detailed process used by an owner to select a consultant to provide planning, design, and other services is unique to each situation. However, steps typically common to the consultant selection process can be identified and linked together as shown in FIGURE 3-3 for the benefit of the potential sole practitioner. You, based on your employment experience, are probably familiar with the process. However, a review may be appropriate to help translate your employee experience in the consultant selection process to what could be your individual practitioner role in that process.

Beginning with "Start," the most formal and involved selection process is the series of Steps 1 through 12 proceeding clockwise around the figure. Various optional shortcuts are possible and are frequently used by owners, especially those in the private sector, as they select consultants.

Consider some of the numerous optional, shorter, and simpler routes through the selection process. For example, the client might move directly from Step 2, identify potential consultants, to Step 5, sending requests for proposals (RFP's), thus

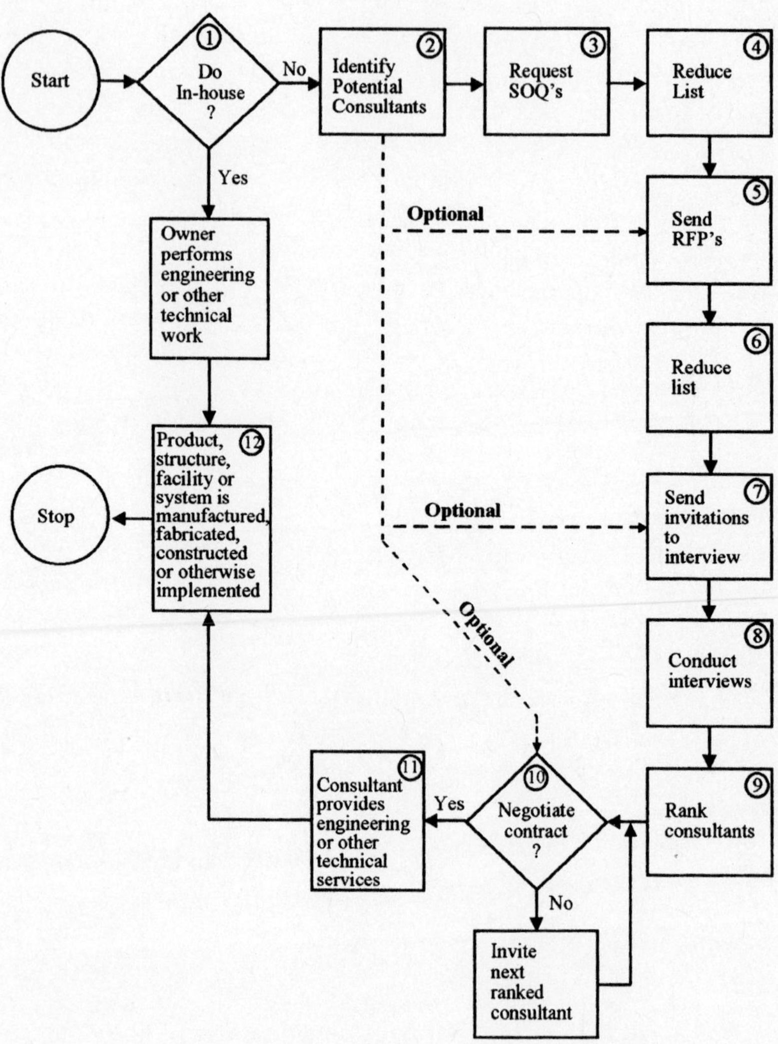

Figure 3-3. While the consultant selection process is unique for each situation, commonalities exist as shown here.

eliminating requesting and reviewing statements of qualifications (SOQ's). An even shorter version of the overall process is to move directly from Step 2, identify potential consultants, to Step 7, extend invitations to interview. This short cut might apply in situations where a client is very familiar with the qualifications of a set of consulting firms and wants to focus immediately on how any one of those firms would form a team and go about doing a particular project. Sometimes, most of the process is omitted, and this is most likely to happen in the private sector, when the client goes from Step 2, identify potential consultants, to Step 10, negotiate a contract. The client makes a predetermination regarding which consultant is most likely to provide the desired services at an acceptable fee and invites that consultant to meet with the client to learn about the project and negotiate a contract.

As noted at the beginning of this chapter, one of the highest compliments that an individual consultant or consulting firm can receive is to be retained on a sole-source basis by a client. As an individual practitioner, a goal of your marketing efforts is to frequently be a sole source selection.

FIGURE 3-3 might be viewed as a client-consultant communication process. The five components of communication (listening, speaking, writing, use of graphics, and use of mathematics) are typically used throughout the consultant selection process. The most qualified consultant may not be selected and the client may be denied the best possible services because of inadequate communication skills on behalf of the consultant, the client, or both.

A final thought is in order on the consultant selection process in the context of marketing of engineering services. As long and complex as the process may be, it is only one component—and a small one at that—of marketing. Chapter 7 is a comprehensive treatment of marketing and provides further context for the consultant selection process.

REVIEW

In closing, reflect on the principal ideas offered in this chapter titled "Roles and Selection of Consultants." While "consultant" could mean a consulting firm, it usually means a particular trusted and competent person—perhaps you. Consultants are typically retained for one or more of the following five reasons: temporarily acquire necessary expertise, supplement in-house staff, provide absolute objectivity, perform unpleasant tasks, and reduce liability. The typically complex consultant selection process is characterized by a tension between quality of service (meeting requirements) and cost of service. The competent person who is trustworthy often enjoys short cuts through the complex consultant selection process. That could be you.

Consider this anonymous closing thought:

> *The bitterness of poor quality remains long after the sweetness of low price is forgotten.*

Chapter 4

Success Factors

For success, attitude is equally important as ability. (Harry F. Banks)

CHARACTERISTICS OF SUCCESSFUL CONSULTANTS

One could argue that of the various employment opportunities for engineers and other technical professionals, consulting is both the most demanding and the most satisfying. The world of the consultant is typically dynamic—new problems to solve, new technologies to learn, new clients to serve and new geographic areas to work in. The dynamics are likely to be the most volatile for the individual practitioner consultant. These exciting attributes of consulting, which are likely to be viewed as positives by many professionals who are "on the outside looking in," must be weighed against potential negatives. These are long hours, erratic schedules, extensive travel, and high levels of stress.

Success in consulting, especially as a sole proprietor, requires the six characteristics shown in FIGURE 4-1. They are:

- **Inquisitiveness and currency of knowledge**

- **Responsiveness to schedules and other needs**

- **Strong people orientation**

- **Self-motivation**

- **Creativity**

1 + 1 = 3

- **Physical and emotional toughness**

Figure 4-1. Successful consultants tend to have these six characteristics.

- **Inquisitiveness and currency of knowledge** — Recall that the consultant is often retained to provide expertise the client does not possess. Consultants, as individuals or as organizations, should define their areas of expertise and remain current in them. On the surface, one might think that consultants are successful primarily because of the answers they provide based on their knowledge and experience. However, the questions they ask their clients, others, and themselves based on their knowledge and experience are more important than the answers they give. Once key questions are asked, the consultant knows how to find the answers. The successful consultant is a ***perpetual student***, strongly oriented towards trying to find out more about his or her area of expertise, the current task or project, the client, and the client's environment. Clearly, the consultant's inquisitiveness spans technical and non-technical subjects and topics.

  Many engineers and other technical professionals have always liked learning. Positive terms like studious, serious, good student, and thinker were applied to them as they progressed through the formal education process. Negative labels have also been used such as egghead, bookworm, nerd, geek, and professional student. However, time has proven that these are positive values.

  The last label, professional student, was increasingly stuck on the author as he continued graduate work while many contemporaries took "real jobs." The low point occurred when he was nearing the end of his formal studies. His grandmother, who never had an unpleasant word for him and had left school after the fifth grade, said "Stuart, what a shame! You are 27 years old and not working." He was so embarrassed!

But, like many of you, he persisted, and now works as an individual practitioner. He is still a professional student but no longer embarrassed. Instead, he is very fortunate! Being a fully functioning individual practitioner means many things, one of which is being a professional student. What are ***you*** studying?

- **Responsiveness to schedules and other needs** – Recall that the consultant may be retained because the client does not have the personnel to complete a task or do a project. If the effort is late because of the consultant, the principal reason for retaining the consultant is negated. Responsiveness to client needs and schedules requires that the consultant have a strong service orientation. Are you service oriented?

- **Strong people orientation** – Although technical professionals plan, design, construct, fabricate, manufacture, and care for "things," they are doing this for the benefit of people. The consultant is a very important part of the interface between the needs of people and the possibilities of meeting those needs with the applications of science and technology. Accordingly, effectiveness in consulting requires a high degree of communication skills, with emphasis on listening, writing, and speaking. The successful consultant enjoys interacting with people, but may find that some are not very pleasant because they are under great personal or organizational stress, or perhaps, because of their basic personality. Inflating the egos of some clients and tolerating the over-inflated egos of others could take a toll on your own ego. But, as suggested by Perlstein (1998, p. 25), "Deflate your ego and you can inflate your income." In a similar vein, he (1998, p. 226) offers this advice: "Thicken your hide and thin out your ego, and you'll fatten your wallet." The people challenges of consulting are further complicated by frequent changes in clients, potential clients and their representatives. Is your skin "thick enough?"

- **Self-motivation** — Even though an individual consultant is "working for" a client, a client often does not know how to direct the consultant or have the time or the inclination to do so. Accordingly, most of what consultants do for clients is at the consultant's initiative within the overall framework established by the consultant-client agreement. Clients tend to assume that if they are not hearing anything from "their consultant," the consultant is proceeding with the project in a timely fashion. Moreover, the consultant must be available, on very short notice, to answer a question, give advice, or provide a status report or other accounting of the efforts to date. Consultants should be highly proactive to the point of being intrusive in their relationships with clients. Are you predisposed to keep things moving ahead?

- **Creativity** — Theodore von Karman, the Hungarian-American aeronautical engineer, said "scientists define what is, engineers create what never has been." Consultants must have the ability to be creative, to synthesize, and to see previously unforeseen patterns and possibilities. The typical technical project involves technical, financial, regulatory, personnel, and other facets, all of which can be easily assembled in a variety of ways most of which are suboptimal. A consultant's combination of knowledge, highly varied experience, and objectivity should enable him or her to suggest approaches and solutions not apparent to others. How creative are you?

- **Physical and emotional toughness** – The successful consultant needs physical and emotional strength to withstand pressure, long hours, and travel. Some of the consultant's meetings and presentations are very difficult because they occur in situations highly charged by personality conflicts, political pressure, financial concerns, and liability issues. In addition, consultants are often not selected for projects even though they believe they were the most qualified or had the best proposal. Frequent rejection can take its toll on conscientious and competent individuals, but is one of the realities of the consulting field. Are you tough enough?

FROM ONE OR A FEW TO MANY "HATS"

Another way of viewing what is needed to be a successful sole proprietor is to consider the functions you must perform and the roles you must fill. If you are employed by a public or private engineering organization, you probably have one or a few principal functions. Perhaps you are a designer, a project manager or a department head. Maybe you are two or even all three of these. Employees typically wear one or a few hats--certainly fewer, however, than the typical individual practitioner.

One of the realities of being a successful, self-employed, free lancer is that you must be able to "wear many hats" and often at the same time. FIGURE 4-2 illustrates the concept of moving from wearing one or a few too many hats. A partial,

NOW, AS AN EMPLOYEE	THEN, AS AN INDIVIDUAL PRACTITIONER

OR
MAYBE

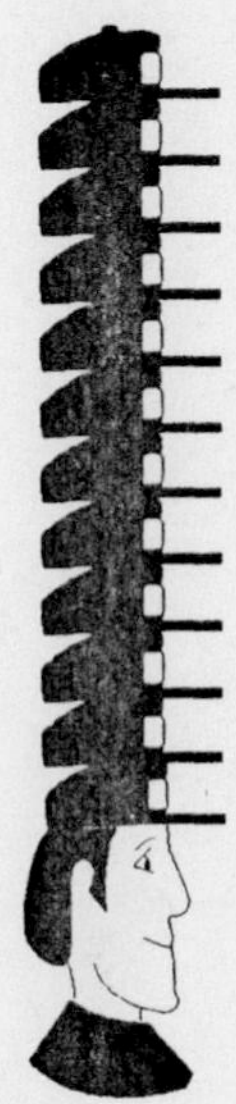

Figure 4-2. Success as an individual practitioner requires "wearing many hats."

alphabetical list of functions that need to be attended to in the typical engineering sole proprietorship is as follows: accountant, chief executive officer (CEO), coach, computer expert, creator, documentor, dreamer, facilitator, friend, integrator, lawyer, listener, marketer, mentor, partner, planner, prime contractor, project engineer, project manager, speaker, subcontractor, teacher, and writer.

Note use of "attended to" in the preceding sentence. Because of the heavy demand on sole practitioners to "wear many hats" and attend to so many matters, some develop mutually beneficial alliances with other sole proprietors or even companies. These alliances, sometimes called virtual teams or virtual organizations, enable a sole proprietor to attend to some of the hats without actually wearing them. The creation of virtual teams is discussed and illustrated in the next chapter under the title of "Team."

Do you have the ability to "wear many hats?" Answering this question and, more broadly, identifying and assessing your personal professional assets is the subject of Chapter 5.

TAKING OFF SOME "HATS"

There are some hats you, as a free lancer, may no longer need to wear. While these are heavily dependent on each situation, you may be able to cast off one or more of the following hats: gopher, outsider, politician, scapegoat, whipping "boy/girl," or "yes" man/woman.

NEGOTIATION: YOUR ATTITUDE AND SKILL

> *If there is any such thing as a wise compromise, it is not likely to be reached by a refusal to think.*
> (Joseph Wood Krutch)

Openness to negotiation and skill in doing it cross over three of the previously discussed success characteristics. Those characteristics are responsiveness to schedules and other needs, strong people orientation, and physical and emotional toughness. Negotiation ability is also essential to carrying out many of the functions discussed under the topic of wearing many more hats. Therefore, success as a free lancer requires a positive attitude towards negotiation and skill in doing it.

Pervasiveness of Negotiating

Gallant (1991, p. 109-110) notes that "...we negotiate whenever we don't have the authority to say 'this is the way this will be done,' or when we have the authority but feel we will achieve better buy-in..." from others. Rarely will you, as a sole proprietor, be in a dictatorial position. You will frequently negotiate with clients, potential clients, team members, subcontractors, suppliers, regulators, and others.

In contrast to individual practitioners, some employees of organizations are in dictatorial positions especially if they still operate under the old command and control philosophy. If you place high value on having your way, and can do so because you hold a command and control position as an employee, stay put. Free lancing, with its attendant pervasive negotiating, is not for you.

Negotiating Paradigms

Covey (1990, pp. 206-220) identifies various paradigms for negotiating or, what he calls, human interaction. Included are:

- "I lose, you lose": This can happen when egos are of top priority and the negotiating parties are vindictive.

- "I win, you lose": Covey notes that most people are "deeply scripted" in this concept. It reflects a scarcity mentality whereas "I win, you win" embodies an abundance mentality.

- "I lose, you win": Appeasers adapt this approach and, according to Covey, "…bury a lot of feelings…" that are eventually manifested in ugly ways.

- "I win, you win or no deal": If lasting, trustful relationships are desired, which they often must be for success as a free lancer, the only viable model is "I win/you win."

The "no deal" condition of the "I win/you win" negotiating paradigm speaks directly to you, as a sole proprietor, working hard to build your relationship-based business. Consider "walking away" from any potential consulting assignment, even in sole source situations, if you cannot begin it in a "I win, you win" mode. Look ahead. If you begin a project with either you or your client having already "lost," won't the "loser" have difficulty dealing with suppressed negative feelings toward the "winner?" Even if the outward and material aspects of the project are successful, the buried negative feelings of the "loser" are likely to remain and prevent future contracts.

Negotiation Tips

There is no formula for negotiating to achieve "I win, you win" results as a sole proprietor. However, some suggested approaches, based in part on Covey (1990, pp. 205-234), Gallant (1994, pp. 109-115) and Gerston (1994), may be offered.

- **Do your homework** – Why do you want what you want? For example, in a contract negotiation with a new client, your desired lump sum fee for a project should be supported by a thorough understanding of client requirements and related project scope and deliverables. Similarly, your argument to your team for pursuing a particular alternative course of action should be supported by an enumeration of its positive and negative impacts compared to other options. In negotiating with a potential subcontractor or vendor, you should have a good idea of going rates and prices for their kinds of services or products.

- **Decide what is most important to you** – Determine your key objectives. Decide what is non-negotiable. Another way of saying this is maintain the ability to say "no deal" and walk away by knowing your absolutes. Depending on the situation, non-negotiables might be your fee, approach to be taken, alternatives to be considered, the schedule, or people to be involved.

- **Deepen your understanding of what is most important to the other party** – Ask many and varied questions. Listen empathetically, that is, hear both the other person's words and sense his/her feelings. Try to identify his or her non-negotiables. Meeting your and the other party's needs is crucial to a win-win outcome. Dawson (1995) tells this story:

  Two people have one orange. They assume the best they can do will be to split the orange down the middle—but as they discuss their needs, they find that one wants the orange for juice, and the other wants the rind for a cake. There needn't be a winner and a loser. Both of them can win.

- **Be honest** – This applies to data and information as well as strong feelings and key objectives. A "win" achieved through dishonesty, if subsequently revealed, is likely to indefinitely sour a relationship. Furthermore, your client is often in communication with your other clients or your potential clients. Bad news travels fast. What's the point of "winning" a battle and "losing" the war?

- **Suppress your ego** – Gallant (1991, p. 110) suggests being "…willing to concede face-saving or prestige aspects if that helps you achieve your goals".

Revisiting "I Win, You Lose"

As noted earlier, "I win, you lose" is one of the available negotiating paradigms. Some published negotiating advice supports this approach. For example, Dawson (1995) refers to "I win, you win" as a myth and, as an alternative, he advocates "power negotiating." Some tactics included in power negotiating are asking for more than you expect to get, never saying yes to the first offer, flinching or gasping on hearing the other party's proposal, faking a review by a higher authority, and providing incorrect information. Dawson's tactics are fundamentally different than the negotiation tips presented earlier. And, they should be because the earlier tactics support "I win, you win" and Dawson's tactics support "I win, you lose." Tactics like Dawson's also do not necessarily apply to the trust-based consulting business.

Your success as a sole proprietor consultant will depend, in part, on your negotiation ability. Developing that ability requires adopting a primary negotiation model and then applying consistent tactics. Two models, "I win, you win" and "I win, you lose," have been discussed. An "I win, you lose" approach may work if your focus is on getting single projects with clients and not on building long-term relationships. If long-term relationships are your goal, then trust must be earned which clearly favors the "I win, you win" paradigm.

REVIEW

In summary, consider the main points in this chapter titled "Success Factors." Six traits are required for success as an individual practitioner. They are: inquisitiveness and currency of knowledge, responsiveness to schedules and other needs, strong people orientation, self-motivation, creativity, and physical and emotional toughness. The sole proprietor wears many more hats than the traditionally employed individual. But, the sole proprietor also gets rid of some undesirable hats. Openness to negotiation and skill in doing it are essential to your success as a free lancer.

A closing thought, offered by William J. H. Boetcker, that suggests continuous personal improvement is the key to success as a sole proprietor:

> *Never mind what others do; do better than yourself, beat your own record from day to day, and you are a success.*

Chapter 5

Assessing Your Assets

Some know the price of everything and the value of nothing. (Anonymous)

THE ORIGINAL "DRAW" FOR YOU

What was your motivation for entering engineering, science or some other technically oriented field? "Go back" to your pre-college or early college experiences. Was it to wear many hats making your living as a sole proprietor? Or was your choice of a major driven more by your desire to use mathematics and science to analyze or create useful things? To what extent did your undergraduate education prepare you for being an individual practitioner?

Chances are, your answers to the preceding questions are probably not encouraging from the perspective of the individual practitioner option you are considering. However, don't be prematurely discouraged, especially if you strongly identify with one or more of the telltale "time to go out on your own" signs described in Chapter 2. Your formal, technically-oriented education has probably been heavily supplemented with many and varied experiences. The sum of those experiences may give you a wealth of assets sufficient to start a sole proprietor consulting business venture.

TYPES OF ASSETS: THREE THINGS YOU "BRING TO THE TABLE"

Three Categories

One way to identify and evaluate your non-monetary assets is to view them as being in one of three categories:

- Your ***skills, knowledge, and characteristics:*** Who you are.
- Your ***network:*** Whom you know, and more importantly, what they really know and think about you.
- ***Your client awareness:*** What you know about client needs/wants.

KNOWLEDGE, SKILLS AND CHARACTERISTICS: WHO YOU ARE

Reflect on the first of the three assets: who you are. Hypothetical examples of knowledge, skills, and characteristics that might be possessed by an experienced engineer or other technical professional are:

- Obtaining federal/state funding for public water/wastewater projects
- Applying continuous simulation hydrologic-hydraulic-water quality computer models

- Managing multi-discipline projects
- Writing reports about largely technical topics for technical and non-technical audiences
- Speaking to varied audiences
- Planning, conducting and following up on meetings
- Creating and using spreadsheets
- Thinking "on your feet"
- Being creative and synergistic
- Exhibiting great persistence
- Empathizing

You get the idea. There is a unique set of knowledge/skills/characteristics similar to the preceding list that defines you—or at least those parts of you that are likely to be relevant to a sole proprietor business. Take the time now to make a preliminary list of your "top ten" knowledge/skill/characteristic items. They are:

1. ______________________________
2. ______________________________
3. ______________________________
4. ______________________________
5. ______________________________
6. ______________________________
7. ______________________________

8. ______________________________________

9. ______________________________________

10. ______________________________________

NETWORK MEMBERS: WHOM YOU KNOW

Consider the second of the three assets: whom you know. Hypothetical examples of possible members of your network are:

- Current co-workers
- Clients of your current employer
- Personnel employed by your current competitors
- Members of professional societies
- Committees on which you serve
- Members of your service clubs/civic organizations/religious groups
- Employees of regulatory agencies
- College friends
- Former professors
- Former students
- Neighbors
- Family members

You get the idea! You know and are known by many people from varied "walks of life." Stop, right now, to create a preliminary list of the "top ten" members of your network. They are:

1. ______________________________
2. ______________________________
3. ______________________________
4. ______________________________
5. ______________________________
6. ______________________________
7. ______________________________
8. ______________________________
9. ______________________________
10. ______________________________

Realistically Assess Your Contacts

Assume you are or recently were an employee of a government entity that used consulting services and that is the sole or principal basis of your contact with consulting firms whom you now view as potential clients or references. Or maybe you are or were an employee of a private firm that used the services of consultants and now view those consultants as potential clients or references.

Be cautious. Because you had a cordial and mutually beneficial business relationship with those consultants does not necessarily mean that they have high regard for your abilities in your past role or in your planned consultant role. What you interpret as such may simply have been their "schmoozing" of you. Realistically assess your contacts (the various members of your network) in light of your new role, that is, as a sole proprietor consultant who plans to provide valued advice to clients.

CLIENT AWARENESS: WHAT YOU KNOW ABOUT CLIENT NEEDS/WANTS

Finally, think about the third of the three assets: what you know about client needs and wants. Examples of current and future ***client needs/wants*** that may be known by an experienced engineer or other technical professional are:

- Improving project management
- Acquiring in-house computer modeling capability
- Becoming more profitable
- Establishing a geographic information system (GIS)
- Complying with the new National Pollution Discharge Elimination System (NPDES) stormwater rules
- Creating a corporate university
- Solving conflicts between personnel in the corporate and branch offices

You get the idea! Your list could be "endless" if you've been alert to the overall environment within the government and private sectors. Take the time now to develop a preliminary list of potential clients and their needs/wants as you understand them. In preparing this list, you might enter a specific client (e.g., Boomtown, U.S.A.) and a specific need/want you are aware of (e.g., funding for major airport expansion). Or, you might list a category of clients (e.g., small consulting firms) and a need/want (e.g., improved success rate on proposals). Your list is:

1. ________________________________
2. ________________________________
3. ________________________________
4. ________________________________
5. ________________________________
6. ________________________________
7. ________________________________
8. ________________________________
9. ________________________________
10. ________________________________

TIME OUT

At this point, if you've filled out, or at least seriously thought about, your three asset lists, you may be pleasantly surprised. Your education and experience may have earned you:

- Favorable knowledge, skills and characteristics
- Membership in a large, varied, potentially helpful network
- Broad and deep awareness of client wants/needs

The next step is to see if there is some individual practitioner business value in your three-part assets. That is, evaluate your assets looking for synergism.

EVALUATING YOUR ASSETS: LOOKING FOR SYNERGISM

Your assets will have value to a sole proprietorship only if there is some ***synergistic connection*** among them that will serve clients. That is, there must be some intersection of who you are, whom you know, and what you know about needs. The intersection concept is illustrated in FIGURE 5-1. Review, using TABLE 5-1, three actual examples of intersections among the three categories of assets that were the basis for contracts obtained by an individual practitioner.

The last seven blank rows in the preceding table are for your use. ***Think about intersections that apply to you.*** Write in some potential personal scenarios that might lead to your first contract as a sole proprietor.

To reiterate, the suggested process is to assess your three assets as a potential sole proprietor. The assets are who you are, whom you know, and what you know about client needs/wants. Your business niche will be synergistically defined by the intersection of these.

At this point, do some more creative thinking about what that niche might be. Maybe your niche is taking on some of the hardest jobs—“work horse” jobs that “show horses” don’t want to touch. On the other hand, because who you are, whom you know, and what you know about needs are each unique to you (there’s nobody else like you), your niche will be unique. Your niche may even appear unconventional, unorthodox, strange, weird or extreme. Do not, at this juncture, necessarily be detoured and take a more conventional path. Ralph Waldo Emerson, in his essay “Self-Reliance” (Emerson, 1936, p. 31), offers this advice:

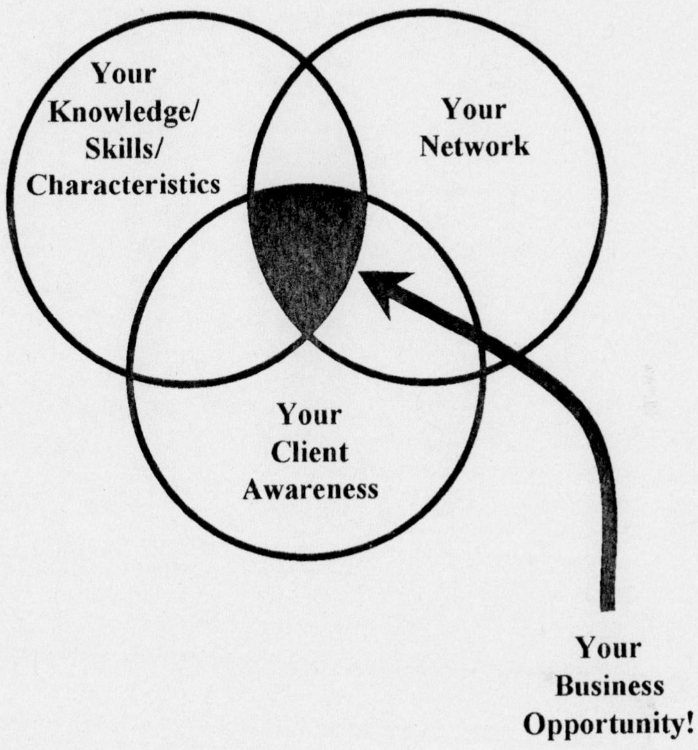

Figure 5-1. Your assets will have value in a sole proprietorship if they intersect.

Table 5-1. Systematically assess who you are, whom you know, and what you know about needs.

Scenario/ Example	Knowledge/ Skills/ Character-istics	Network	Client Need/ Want	Result
1.	• Knowledge about stormwater manage-ment • Writing/ editing ability	• U.S. Environ-mental Protec-tion Agency (USEPA) research and develop-ment (R&D) person • Several storm-water manage-ment experts	• Technical review and editing of a draft storm-water manage-ment report	Contract to provide review/ editing services

Table 5-1. Systematically assess who you are, whom you know, and what you know about needs.

2.	• Knowledge of corporate universities (CU) • Knowledge of traditional university curricula, administration, and faculty	• Former member of CU client firm • Current member of CU client	• Outside review of proposed CU	Contract to provide on-site review/ advice
3.	• In-depth understanding of consulting engineering business • Good and bad project management (PM) experiences • Researching and writing skill • Presentation skill	• Members of existing client firm	• Make $ on projects	Contracts to prepare PM handbook and conduct two PM workshops

Table 5-1. Systematically assess who you are, whom you know, and what you know about needs.

4.				
5.				
6.				

Table 5-1. Systematically assess who you are, whom you know, and what you know about needs.

7.				
8.				
9.				
10.				

> *A man should learn to detect and watch that gleam of light which flashes across his mind from within, more than the lustre of the firmament of bards and sages. Yet he dismisses without notice his thought, because it is his. In every work of genius, we recognize our own rejected thoughts; they come back to us with a certain alienated majesty.*

Past is not necessarily prologue. As an employee of one or more organizations, you may have filled primarily technical functions but, in the process, acquired insight into many and varied, non-technical, management-related issues. This knowledge, combined with whom you know and what you know about client needs, may synergistically enable you to become a management consultant to technically-oriented organizations. You know what they do and the non-technical challenges they face.

As you contemplate potential synergistic business niches, give thought to the kind of people you are most likely to work with as clients. For example, if your sole proprietorship offers technical services, you will probably interact with middle level, technically-oriented managers in consulting firms or government agencies. If, in contrast, you decide to focus on non-technical, management-related services, you are most likely to interact with CEO's and other upper level executives.

List here some one-sentence descriptions of service niches you, and perhaps you alone, might fill as a sole proprietor:

____

____

____

____

FILLING IN GAPS: TEN TIPS

What about gaps, weaknesses, and liabilities in our assets? Assume that your determination and evaluation of personal assets is encouraging, but there are some gaps:

- Maybe you lack some seemingly critical knowledge/skills/characteristics.
- Perhaps your network is a bit small or lacking in certain types of members.
- Possibly there are gaps in your awareness of client needs/wants.

Well, welcome to the club! Nobody is 100% prepared to "go out on their own." No one has, or even will have, 100% of the necessary personal assets to get into or stay in the sole proprietor business. However, you can reduce your liabilities (while leveraging your assets) in many and varied ways. Ten specific suggestions follow.

Study Business Related Topics

Identify and prioritize your knowledge and skill gaps in technical and non-technical areas. Search for ways to close those gaps. Read articles, papers, and books; listen to audio tapes; view videos; take courses at the local university or over the web; and attend seminars. Incidentally, now you will be paying the entire cost of your continuing education—money and time! You may be surprised to find out how much more you get out of these learning situations. Skim the References and Bibliography sections of this book for articles, papers and books. In addition to this book, note the books by Holtz, Lindeburg, and Perlstein which focus on sole proprietors.

Read Eclectically

> *A man is known by the company his mind keeps.* (Thomas Bailey Aldrich, Author)

One way to broaden your knowledge and stimulate your thinking is to regularly read materials drawn from outside of your normal reading patterns and not necessarily related to work. For example, if you don't normally do so, occasionally read newspapers such as the *Christian Science Monitor, Financial Times, Investors Business Daily* (Note: Read the "Leaders and Success" section which, each day, features one of *IBD's* "10 Secrets to Success"), *Wall Street Journal* and *New York Times* and magazines and other periodicals such as *Fortune*, *Money, National Review* and *The Economist*.

Expand your reading to books that are not narrowly focused on business or technical subjects. Consider, for example, some of the following:

- *Think and Grow Rich* by Napoleon Hill (Fawcett, 1960). This book has a somewhat misleading title. It does not, as perhaps suggested by the title, focus on accumulation of material wealth but does stress achieving ambitious aspirations. Hill's research into the lives of many highly accomplished people, as detailed in his book, convinced him of the power of visualization in combination with the workings of the subconscious mind.

- *As A Man Thinketh* by James Allen (Peter Pauper Press, no date). This thoughtful, little book argues, consistent with Napoleon Hill's thesis, that we become what we think, positive or negative, through the power of our subconscious.

- *7 Habits of Highly Effective People* by Stephen Covey (Simon & Schuster, 1990). Unlike many of the gimmicky self-help books, Covey's focuses on application of sound personal and interpersonal principles.

- *First You Have to Row A Boat* by Richard Bode (Warner Books, 1993). Sailing is used as an insightful analogy to life.

Experience indicates that eclectic reading may provide a fresh perspective on tried and true processes; offer a glimpse of future technologies and service needs; expand your vocabulary; provide added insight into human nature; and introduce you to potential business partners. Plotinus, the Roman philosopher, said it this way: "All things are filled full of signs, and it is a wise man who can learn about one thing from another."

Join or Communicate With Carefully Selected Professional and Business Organizations

Select one or a few organizations that will help you learn and possibly network. Be actively involved in at least one of them. For example, serve on a technical committee, present a paper or chair a conference session. Rub elbows with, learn from and get to know leaders. Adopt a passive role in other organizations while benefiting from their publications and other services. Presented here is information on some professional and business organizations that may be useful to the engineer sole proprietor:

AMERICAN SOCIETY OF CIVIL ENGINEERS

Address:

ASCE
1801 Alexander Bell Drive
Reston, VA 20191-2723

http://www.pubs.asce.org/
Tel: 1-800-548-2723

Publications:

Journal of Management in Engineering: This bi-monthly journal contains numerous articles on marketing, communication, project management, and other topics likely to be of interest to the individual practitioner. An additional potentially helpful ASCE journal, *Leadership and Management in Engineering*, will debut in the first quarter of 2001.

NATIONAL ASSOCIATION FOR THE SELF-EMPLOYED

Address:

National Association for the Self-Employed
1023 15th Street NW, Suite 1200
Washington, DC 20005-2600

Tel: 1-800-232-6273
Fax: 1-202-466-2123
http://www.nase.org/

Purpose:

Quoted from NASE's web page: "The NASE represents more than 325,000 self-employed Americans and owners of very small businesses nationwide. The organization has grown steadily to become the largest association of our kind. Membership spans a wide range of businesses, notably in the retail, service, construction and consulting fields. Most are 'very' small, small firms with over 85% having fewer than five employees."

Publication:

Self-Employed America: This bi-monthly publication provides information about topics such as national, issues, taxes, finance, and management.

U.S. SMALL BUSINESS ADMINISTRATION AND SMALL BUSINESS DEVELOPMENT CENTERS

Address:

U.S. Small Business Administration
409 3rd St. S. W.
Washington, D.C. 20416

Tel: 1-800-827-5722
Fax: 202-205-7064
http://www.sbaonline.sba.gov/

Purpose:

Quoted from the SBA's web site: "The U.S. Small Business Administration

(SBA) administers the Small Business Development Center (SBDC) Program to provide management assistance to current and prospective small business owners. SBDCs offer one-stop assistance to small businesses by providing a wide variety of information and guidance in central and easily accessible branch locations. The program is a cooperative effort of the private sector, the educational community and federal, state and local governments. It enhances economic development by providing small businesses with management and technical assistance. There are now 57 small business development centers—one in every state (Texas has four), the District of Columbia, Guam, Puerto Rico and the U.S. Virgin Islands—with a network of nearly 1,000 service locations. In each state there is a lead organization which sponsors the SBDC and manages the program. The lead organization coordinates program services offered to small businesses through a network of subcenters and satellite locations in each state. Subcenters are located at colleges, universities, community colleges, vocational schools, chambers of commerce and economic development corporations."

ILISE BENUN, CONSULTANT

Address:

Ilise Benun
P. O. Box 23
Hoboken, NJ 07030-0023

Tel: 1-800-737-0783
Fax: 201-222-2494
Email: mailto:dovit@connext.net
http://www.artofselfpromotion.com

Publication:

The Art of Self Promotion: This quarterly newsletter is "...dedicated to the integration of creativity and integrity in business and is committed to providing ideas and resources for manageable marketing to fit our busy lives."

Other publications and products are available.

SMALL BUSINESS COMPUTING AND COMMUNICATION AND HOME OFFICE COMPUTING

Address:

http://www.smalloffice.com/

Description:

As also noted in Chapter 6, the two named monthly magazines maintain this website. It contains useful information and provides access to a free weekly email newsletter.

Access Useful Websites

The preceding listing of professional and business organizations included their websites. Other websites oriented to sole proprietors or small businesses are:

- http://www.allbusiness.com/ (click on Entrepreneur Center)
- http://www.bCentral.com (provides ideas on connecting your business to the web, marketing online, and addressing management issues)
- http://www.freeagent.com/ (a comprehensive site for freelancers)
- http://www.nolo.com/ (a self-help law center for the small businesses)
- http://www.pathfinder.com/fortune/ (click on Small Business)
- http://www.quicken.com/small_business (another comprehensive site for the sole proprietor)
- http://www.sbaonline.sba.gov/starting/businessplan.html (outlines the elements of a business plan)
- http://www.workingsolo (serves the rapidly growing SOHO, that is, small office/home office, market)

Subscribe to E-Newsletters

Electronic newsletters, most of which are available at no cost, can provide another way to learn more of what you need to be a successful individual practitioner. Examples of free, short, informative, no nonsense e-newsletters are:

- *1099 E-Newsletter:* To subscribe to this free weekly newsletter for independent professionals, send an email to listbot@1099.com.
- *Free Agent Nation Newsletter:* To subscribe to this free newsletter, go to http://www.freeagentnation.com/newsstand/newsletter.html.
- *Geoff's Gems:* To subscribe to this free newsletter go to http://www.garage.com/geoffsGems.shtml.
- *QUICKEN.COM NEWSLETTER*: To subscribe to this free monthly newsletter, go to http://www.omm.com/cg/quicken.cgi?source=stuwalesh@aol.com.
- *SalesDoctorsMagazine:* To subscribe to this free weekly, sales-oriented newsletter go to http://salesdoctors.com/misc/subscribe.htm.
- *Smalloffice.com's Bizwire*: To subscribe to this free weekly newsletter, send an email to smalloffice-3616@mailsubs.com.
- *SmartBiz News:* To subscribe to this bi-monthly newsletter go to http://www.smartbiz.com.
- *Working Solo eNews:* To subscribe to this free monthly newsletter go to http://www.workingsolo.com/newsletter.

Learn On Projects

Set a goal of learning on each project you do, that is, learn while you earn. This will be an easy-to-achieve goal! More specifically, seek out projects that, while they will draw primarily on your areas of competency, will enable you to learn in your areas of deficiency.

An example is in order. Assume you, as a sole practitioner, are an expert in the design of improvements at small, general aviation airports. You know all about the Federal Aviation Administration (FAA) design circulars. Many of your designs have been constructed and are in use. This is very satisfying. However, you would like to learn more about how airport improvements are financed. One way to do this, as a sole practitioner, would be to join a team that is responsible for all aspects, including financing, of an airport project. As you productively contribute your expertise to the efforts of the project team, you can learn about financing from the team member who has that expertise.

Caveat: Learning on the job, that is, seeking assignments that will fill in knowledge or skill gaps, is potentially problematic in two ways. First, you could risk making errors or allowing omissions. This could be costly, both monetarily and in terms of your reputation.

Second, engineering and other codes of ethics require professionals to practice only in their areas of competence. You could risk an ethical violation or the appearance of one. For example, the second of seven Fundamental Canons in the Code of Ethics of the American Society of Civil Engineers (ASCE, 1998) states that "Engineers shall perform services only in areas of their competence." This canon is supported by three very explicit "guidelines." These guidelines (direct quotes) are:

- Engineers shall undertake to perform engineering assignments only when qualified by education or experience in the technical field of engineering involved.

- Engineers may accept an assignment requiring education or experience outside of their own fields of competence, provided their services are restricted to those phases of the project in which they are qualified. All other phases of such project shall be performed by qualified associates, consultants or employees.

- Engineers shall not affix their signatures or seals to any engineering plan or document dealing with subject matter in which they lack competence by virtue of education or experience or to any such plan or document not reviewed or prepared under their supervisory control.

In summary, be competent in your core functions on a project. Restrict your learning to the fringes.

Team

An article (*Economist*, June, 1999) about the business impact of the internet and other newer technologies draws this conclusion:

> *The boundaries of companies will also change... Companies will find it easier to outsource and to use communications to develop deeper relations with suppliers, distributors and many others who might once have been vertically integrated into the firm. Indeed, vertical integration is likely to become less attractive; instead, the diplomatic art of managing ad hoc partnerships and alliances will become a key executive skill.*

The preceding suggests another way to fill in gaps and compensate for your deficiencies in knowledge, skills, characteristics, contacts, or client intelligence; that is join with others—form an ad hoc partnership or a team—for client or project specific purposes. More precisely, form a virtual project team. A virtual project team is a temporary gathering of a prime sole proprietor plus several sole proprietors and other entities organized to meet the requirements of a particular client or project. Although employed in a variety of organizations and functions in various locations, team members are usually linked electronically to achieve a well-defined purpose. Once that purpose is accomplished, the team is likely to disband, never to be re-assembled in exactly the same manner. Some team members may have worked together on a virtual team in the past and others may work together in the future—but only if driven by client or project requirements. FIGURE 5-2 is an example of an actual virtual project team. Members of this team never before functioned as indicated. They were brought together by circumstances and the need to meet client requirements.

The client may or may not be aware of the distinction between being served by a traditional, in-organization project team versus a virtual project team. If the client shows interest, they have a right to know how they are being served. However, in most cases the test of the delivery system will not be "how they are organized." Instead, the test will be "how do they perform" on the three part deliverables, schedule and budget stage.

Ashton and Ashton (1999) offers several suggestions for effective functioning of a virtual team. Some are particularly relevant.

- First, "work only with people you know and trust." Test the waters with a small project.

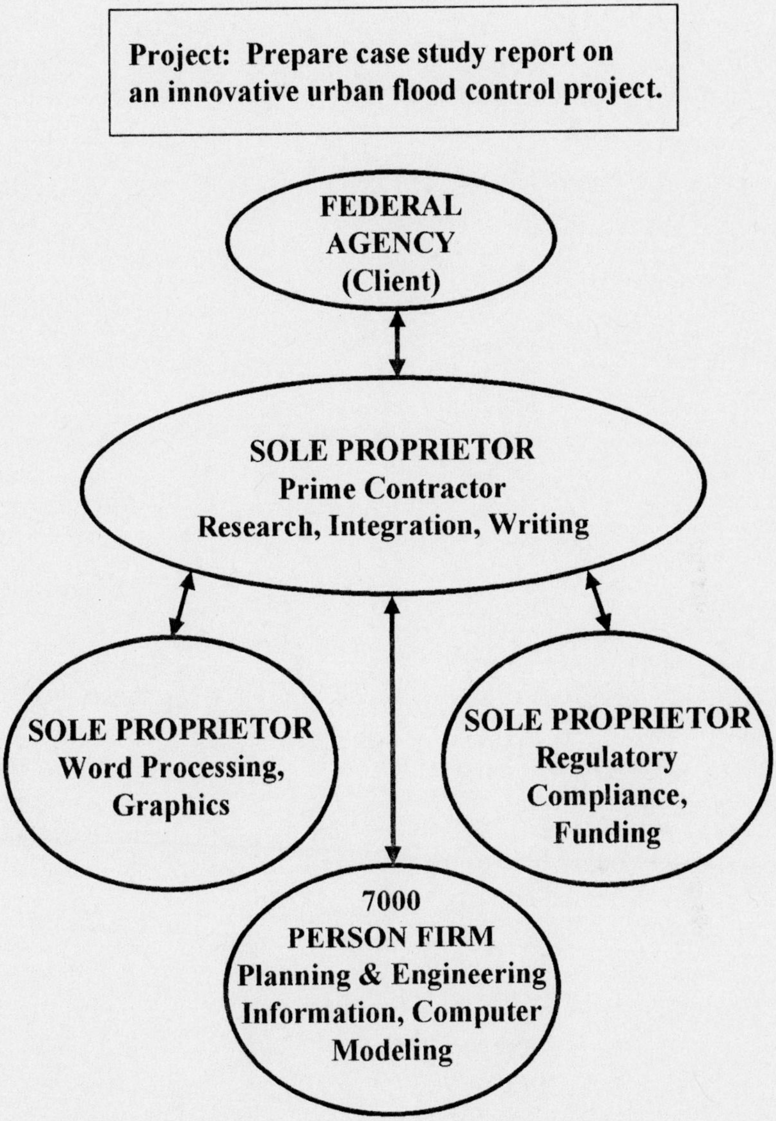

Project: Prepare case study report on an innovative urban flood control project.

Figure 5-2. Example of a virtual project team.

- Second, clearly define up front, in writing, and for each team member, the scope of services, schedule, deliverables and budgets. That is, prepare a project plan as is strongly advocated in Chapter 9.

- Third, establish a communication protocol. For example, select the primary mode of communication recognizing that there are many options including telephone, fax, email, pagers and websites. With email and website communication, costs are independent of distance, unlike telephone and fax communication. The selection of members for a virtual team and the ease and cost of communication among them should not be hindered by distances among them. Email and website communication supports this principle.

Outsource

Just as clients retain you for your expertise, you should consider retaining other specialists for their expertise. Even if you have the necessary expertise, outsourcing some tasks may make more business sense.

When you are doing billable work for a client, outsourcing costs can usually be passed on to the client. In fact, outsourcing certain tasks at an hourly rate less than yours could result in less costs to the client. Depending on the nature of the agreement between you and the client (e.g., lump sum), outsourcing could result in more net revenue for you. You may also want to outsource some non-billable tasks or functions. Possible reasons include your lack of the necessary expertise or your time can be more productively used elsewhere.

As an alternative to outsourcing, Binsacca (2000) suggests bartering for expertise. No money changes hands. You provide your expertise to another sole proprietor and he or she provides an equal value of expertise to you. Look around your network for possibilities.

Consider this example. You are a competent writer. Someone in your network is skilled with graphics. You devote four hours to writing or editing his or her report and, in return, you earn four hours (or some other pre-agreed equivalent amount) of graphic services.

Form Your Own Board of Directors

So you've assessed your assets. How do things look? You think things "look good" but you have some doubts. Nothing unusual here! How about forming and utilizing your own "Outside Board of Directors?" Step back from your current "job" and all those people—within and outside of your organization—who seem so visible and vital now. Examples might be your boss, the head of the other departments whose work products you need, and client representatives. Instead, think more broadly, more expansively. Get beyond your immediate, day-to-day professional and business "got-to-stay-in-touch" contacts. As you cast your "net," who might be able to help you? How about?

- Former "bosses." They typically know you very well.
- Your pastor, rabbi, priest, or other spiritual advisor. Years ago, the author bought lunch for his pastor and sought advice concerning an opportunity to make a marked position change within engineering. Although the pastor knew essentially nothing about engineering, he apparently knew much about "gut

driven" change impulses. His advice was something like this: "If your desire to make such a big change persists, in frequency and intensity, you'd better do it—go with the flow." The author made a major change, partly in keeping with his pastor's advice, and that change opened many doors and in unexpected directions.

- Your financial advisor who, although he thinks an "engineer" is someone who "drives a train," seems to know something about leveraging assets—monetary or otherwise.

- Trusted work colleagues who have the ability to see you outside of the narrow context of work.

- Former college professors.

You are not likely to ever convene a meeting of your entire "board." However, they may be available on an individual basis to provide seasoned advice.

Re-invent Yourself

> *In truth, the only difference between those who have failed and those who have succeeded lies in the difference of their habits. Good habits are the key to all success... I will form good habits and become their slave. (Mandino, 1968, p. 54)*

This means of compensating for weakness is most applicable to deficiencies in personal characteristics, not in knowledge/skill, networking or awareness of client needs/wants.

It is also most difficult to achieve because it requires a high degree of commitment and self discipline. Simply stated, if your personal attitudes are seriously at odds with your success as a sole proprietor, drop the idea of going on your own or decide to markedly change yourself. For example:

- Diminish your need for order and accept ambiguity.

- Balance your reliance on data and logic with increased confidence in your intuition.

- Replace finding "reasons why it can't be done" with "finding ways to do it."

- Diminish risk aversion while increasing opportunity thinking. As some one (anonymously) said: "Don't be afraid to go out on a limb. That's where the fruit is."

- Force yourself from introversion to extraversion

- Revamp your wardrobe. "O wad some power the giftie gie us to see oursels as ithers see us!" (Robert Burns, 1759-1796, Scottish poet, in "To A Louse").

- Stop telling and start asking.

- Read widely and eclectically, not narrowly and technically.

- Stop trying to figure out everything for yourself and, instead, see a counselor, take a personality test (e.g., the Myers-Briggs Type Indicator which will classify you into one of 16 personality types), or have a personal coach (*Modern Maturity*, 2000).

- Stop plugging away and, instead, take a sabbatical to find yourself.
- Seek first to understand and then to be understood (Covey, 1990).
- View these as the ten most powerful, two letter words in the world: ***If it is to be, it is up to me.***

GEOGRAPHICALLY NEUTRAL, EASILY TRANSPORTABLE BUSINESS

To the extent you want to and can, design your sole proprietorship to be geographically neutral and easily transportable. Consider these definitions:

- Geographically Neutral: Most of the time—say 90% or more—you devote to a typical client is offsite, that is, not at their place. You are working for them and serving them well but not physically with them. Assume, for example, that you offer specialty design services and typically function as a member of the client's design team. You are likely to be tied to your client's location(s) a large fraction of the time. Your individual practitioner business is not geographically neutral. Or maybe you plan to do computer hardware and software troubleshooting. Again, you are likely to be tied to your clients' locations. In contrast, if you are only occasionally on-site at your clients' offices and interact primarily by telephone, email, fax, etc., then your free lance business is geographically neutral. Thanks largely to electronic communication devices, geographically neutral sole proprietorships are easy to establish.

- Readily Transportable: Essentially everything you need to conduct your business, that is, your office, can be relocated with little effort. If, for example, you provide laboratory services, your business is probably not readily transportable. In contrast, the typical consulting business files and even basic office equipment can be readily relocated.

A geographically neutral individual practitioner business is desirable because of the options it offers you. Such a business permits you to work in your home office or home base most of the time thus minimizing downtime and stress. A geographically neutral business also allows you to do some productive work while traveling for business or for business and pleasure. A geographically neutral business can also be conducted from some remote, but attractive location such as a mountain cabin, seaside home, or boat.

A free lance business that is both geographically neutral and easily transportable offers the advantage of being able to regularly relocate for extended periods. For example, you may want to eventually have two homes and spend summers in the north and winters in the south. This option will not be available if you are tightly tied to your client's places of business or a single location of your equipment and facilities.

Now, during the formative stage of your sole proprietorship, is the time to keep future options open. Now is the time to design a geographically neutral, easily transportable business.

MONETARY ASSETS

Self Financing

When speaking of assets, monetary ones naturally come to mind. That is, those things that can be measured in dollars and cents. The good news about starting a sole proprietorship in engineering and allied technical and non-technical service fields is that you need little capital to get started. Start up equipment and supplies are discussed in Chapter 6. If you buy all the equipment and supplies you need, which is unlikely, because you probably already have some necessities, the monetary outlay needed to start a free lance business is small. It can easily be done for several thousand dollars. The major financial challenge may be monetary resources to live on while you build your business. Advice on net worth and estimating business income and expenses in your first year is presented in Chapter 10.

External Financing

Although rare for the sole proprietor consultant start-up, you may want a loan. If so, consider doing one or more of the following:

- Contact the closest SBDC office of the SBA. Refer to the earlier discussion in this chapter of the SBA and the SBDC. The SBDC will provide advice, not loans.

- Contact your bank. Most banks will have an interest in helping you succeed so that you become/remain a customer.

- Contact the SBA at http://www.sba.gov. The SBA does not make loans but they do back loans that may be considered too risky by local banks.

For additional ideas on start-up loans and grants, refer to McKimmie (2000).

TOO MUCH OF A GOOD THING

> *I wasted time, and now time doth*
> *waste me.* (Shakespeare)

The premise of this chapter, which is titled "Assessing Your Assets," is as stated beginning on the first page:

> *Your formal, technically-oriented education has probably been heavily supplemented with many and varied experiences. The sum of those experiences may give you a wealth of assets sufficient to start a sole proprietor business venture.*

After assessing your assets, with emphasis on their experiential basis, you may decide that you are not quite ready to fly solo. A little more experience is needed. Be careful! Experience gives us the ability and confidence to take on new challenges. Thoughtfully applied, experience also helps us learn from and not repeat mistakes, although this doesn't necessarily always follow. As someone said "experience is wonderful, it helps us recognize a mistake the second time we make it." While more experience might be useful, recognize that you will never have enough. Furthermore, the value of experience lies in its depth and breadth, that is, its quality and not the quantity as measured, for example, in years or the number of times you have done a particular type of project. Finally, the "I need more experience" idea may be a rationale for not moving ahead.

While experience is valuable, too much of one kind of experience can hamper individual growth. Accordingly, each of us should appraise professional assets at least once a year partly to assess the quality of and freshness of our experience. This evaluation of professional assets might be in the form of a resume update exercise. What new areas of technology have been mastered? What new management techniques were used? What new concepts, ideas, or principles were studied? What new skills were acquired? What new challenges and responsibilities were accepted? What new opportunities were seized and new risks taken? What knowledge was shared with professional colleagues? What new contributions were made? In what ways have we been "good and faithful servants" with our talents?

As you review several annual accountings of your professional experience, will you find several years each filled with new experiences? Or will you find one year of experience repeated several times? If the latter is true, you may be in the midst of a devastating professional assets "stock market crash."

Resist the temptation to settle into the comfort of routine, rationalizing it in the name of gaining more experience. Og Mandino (1968, p. 53), in his book, *The Greatest Salesman in the World* offers this warning about excessive experience:

> *I will commence my journey unencumbered with either the weight of unnecessary knowledge or the handicap of meaningless experience... In truth, experience teaches thoroughly yet her course of instruction devours men's years so the value of her lessons diminishes with the time necessary to acquire her special wisdom.*

Individuals who have had too much of one kind of experience by being in the same or similar situations for a long time—decade or more—tend to be least prepared and most reluctant to set up a sole proprietorship. Three examples of how a person might be in the same or similar situation for a long time—too long a time—are:

- Working for the same organization for two or more decades, even with occasional changes in function and responsibility.

- Spending decades in either government, education or consulting. For example, civil engineers, among all engineers, are positioned by their education and their responsibility in society to work in all three sectors. Having served in two or three sectors enriches their experience and prepares them to become individual practitioners.

- Focusing on one function, regardless of employer, for too long. Examples are being a designer, construction manager, marketer, or administrator for two or more decades.

The comfort that comes with repetition and routine exacts a cost. It narrows one's breadth and wealth of experience and, therefore, one's potential as a free lancer. Using a sailing metaphor, Richard Bode in *First You Have to Row A Little Boat* (Warner, 1993, p. 51) gives this advice:

> *The frantic individual tacks too soon, jumping from job to job... The obtuse individual remains on the same tack too long, investing too much time, talent and energy in a course that takes him far from his avowed objectives. But the seasoned sailor stays on the same tack as long as it appears advantageous, and then...deftly changes directions...the confirmed sailor goes on tacking forever.*

Each of us has opportunities to deftly change direction so that we gain new and valuable professional experience and, as a result, more autonomy, higher income, and greater satisfaction. Examples of ways to acquire asset-building experience include asking for new job assignments, requesting a transfer to another part of your organization, seeking a new employer, returning to school, becoming active in a professional or business organization, and establishing a sole proprietorship. In the final analysis, each of us has his or her hand on the tiller. Maybe you already have enough experience to use the tiller to set a course toward becoming an individual practitioner.

REVIEW

In closing, reflect on the principal ideas offered in this chapter titled "Assessing Your Assets." Your formal education probably did not prepare you to become an individual practitioner. However, your experience may have. You bring three assets to the sole proprietorship table: who you are; whom you know, that is your network; and what you know about client needs/wants. Your three assets have value to a free lance business if they intersect, that is, if they combine synergistically to meet the needs of clients. Assume that your evaluation of personal assets is promising, but there are some gaps in skills, knowledge or contacts. Ways to close those gaps include study of business-related topics, eclectic reading, joining professional and business organizations, learning on projects, teaming, forming a board of directors and re-inventing yourself. Consider establishing a geographically neutral, easily transportable business. Caution: Don't fall into the "I need more experience" trap. The value of experience lies in its depth and breadth, not duration. Quality, not quantity, is the key. Monetary assets are much less important than personal assets to the potential individual practitioner. You will need very little capital to get started. However, you may need monetary resources to live on while you build your business.

Consider this closing thought from an anonymous source:

> *Find a life's work you enjoy, and you will never work another day in your life.*

Chapter 6

Logistics of Getting Started

Get your ducks in a row.
(Anonymous)

SOME "NUTS AND BOLTS"

Assume you have, or soon will have, your first contract. The time to produce—to provide deliverables on time and within budget—is imminent. If you haven't done so already, you will need to establish an office and equip it. For income tax purposes, you need to select a legal form of ownership for your free lance business. Finally, your business needs a name. This chapter offers relevant suggestions under the topics of:

- Office in or outside of your home?
- Equipment and supplies
- Making it legal: selecting a form of ownership
- What's in a name?

- Something's missing!

OFFICE IN OR OUTSIDE OF YOUR HOME?

Because of the recent development of cost-effective electronic devices (e.g., fax machines, personal computers, "beepers," digitizers, wireless telephones) and related services (e.g., overnight mail, websites, voicemail, and call forwarding), you are very likely to find a home office to be technically feasible. Frankly, you can buy all the basic equipment you need, including furniture, for several thousand dollars. A decade or so ago, a home office would probably not have been technically feasible for most sole proprietors. However, technical feasibility is not the only consideration in deciding where your office should be. Four likely decision factors are shown in FIGURE 6-1 and discussed here:

- Cost: A ***home office will be much less costly than an outside office*** assuming you have available space in your home. With the home office, you avoid costs like rent, commuting, and purchasing and maintaining some business clothing. You may derive monetary benefits such as being able to deduct, from your income, a fraction of utility and other homeowner costs as business expenses.

- Professional Impression: An ***outside office will usually make a better, more business-like impression*** if you meet with clients, business partners and suppliers in your office. However, many sole proprietors never or rarely have such meetings in their offices. Face-to-face meetings are held in the offices of others or in neutral places such as restaurants and

COST

PROFESSIONAL IMPRESSION

CONFLICT WITH HOME LIFE

LEGAL CONSIDERATIONS

Figure 6-1. Consider these factors in deciding if your office should be in your home or outside of your home.

hotels. (From a learning perspective, you will usually gain more value from meeting in their office rather than in your office.) Some more elaborate home offices have separate, outside entrances so that they provide a very good professional impression.

- Conflict with Home Life: A ***home office is much more likely to conflict with home life***, that is, have an intrusive or negative impact on spouse, children and other family members. For example, they may be asked to "be quiet," stay out of certain areas and not answer the telephone or answer it in a certain way. Furthermore, having the office "right there" may create or encourage the workaholic. Approaches such as additional telephone lines, closed doors and designated "office hours" may mitigate some of the negative impacts of a home office on home life.

- Legal Considerations: ***Local zoning and other regulations may prohibit or restrict use of your home as an office***. Depending on the locale, you may be subject to regulations that prohibit certain types of businesses, limit how much of your home can be used for business, prevent you from constructing an office addition or a separate office structure, require a business license, or impose an annual business tax (Washington, 1999).

  Georgia (1999) notes that "...home-based businesses are subject to regulations, licensing requirements, and zoning laws." According to Georgia, regulations and zoning laws applicable to home-based businesses may prohibit certain businesses, limit the amount of space devoted to the business, specify provision of off-street parking, limit employees to individuals in residence, and restrict signage. Bottom line: check first. Contact City Hall or other local government offices. For information on state licenses that may be required, go to the Cornell Law Library's State Statutes website at http://www.law.cornell.edu/topics/state_statute.html.

After considering the preceding pros and cons of home and outside offices, you may decide that eventually you want an attractive outside office. However, primarily for cost reasons, you will start with a home office. If so, you will be in good company. For example, in 1937, Bill Hewlett and David Packard started Hewlett Packard with $538 in a Palo Alto, CA garage (Forbes ASAP, 1999, p. 22; http://www.hp.com). Stephen Jobs and Steve Wozniak, working in a garage in 1975, created the first Apple computer (Barker, 1989, pp. 91-96, Cypert, 1993, pp. 131-132).

Perhaps you've decided on a long-term home office and are thinking about making a significant investment by creating an office in unfinished space (e.g., in the attic of your home) or by "adding on" to your home. Ultimately, this may be the best course of action. However, consider this suggestion: First, set up a temporary office in an existing space. Work there temporarily and, in the process, learn:

- What equipment you need
- Where you want it located relative to your needs
- Lighting requirements
- Desk, storage and space requirements.

Then, with that experience-based knowledge under your belt, design and build your "perfect" home office.

EQUIPMENT AND SUPPLIES

A visit to the local office supply store or, even more convincingly, your Staples, Office Max, or Office Depot will suggest that there is "no end" to available office equipment and supplies. However, what are the basics for the new sole proprietor? A dozen suggestions follow:

1. ***Desk and Chair*** – Your first desk may be the kitchen table, dining room table, a folding table, or a plain hollow core door supported by two-drawer file cabinets.

2. ***File Cabinets/Storage Space/Bookshelves*** – You might start with cardboard banker's boxes or plastic crates.

3. ***Computer and Printer*** – Perhaps you already own one. Consider getting a laptop so that when you travel, you can do word processing, spreadsheet work, email, and access websites.

4. ***Software*** – Basics include word processing and spreadsheet programs. Other useful software tools are a presentation package (e.g., Powerpoint or Corel Draw), project management software (e.g., Microsoft Project), a computer aided drafting and design (CADD) package, personal information manager (e.g., Microsoft Outlook) and the most valuable software could be an anti-virus program.

5. ***Fax Machine*** – This might be part of a multifunctional peripheral that provides faxing, printing, digitizing and copying functions.

6. ***Extra Telephone Line(s)*** – You should dedicate one line to your fax machine and computer modem and another to the telephone. Consider having separate lines for your business. Use a voicemail system, not an answering machine. Voicemail advantages include a more professional sound and no busy signal.

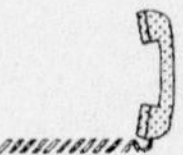

7. ***Wireless (Cellular or Similar) Telephone*** – If you are frequently out of your office, and some sole proprietors are, a wireless telephone is essential. Ask lots of performance and cost questions because this technology is changing very rapidly. For example, the now expensive satellite telephones will eventually come down in price.

8. ***Pager (Beeper)*** – This is needed by a minority of individual practitioners. It may be part of a wireless telephone. Business people are rarely neutral on pagers. They either "love" them, because they can be reached at any time or place or they "hate" them because they can be reached at any time or place. If you are in the latter category, consider having a pager but limiting the number of individuals who have your access number.

9. ***Copy Machine*** –

This is usually not initially needed but may be useful for certain free lancers. For example, you may frequently need to make copies from bound books, journals and magazines. Or you may have to produce relatively large volumes of high quality copies such as needed for seminars. However, don't rule out taking this kind of work to the local copying shop.

10. ***Business Cards and Stationary*** –

These items should be well designed, printed on quality stock and informative (e.g., address, telephone, fax, email, and services offered). Avoid very small print and be sure that your materials copy well.

11. ***Supplies*** -

Stock up on paper, file folders, postage, etc.

12. ***Good Lighting, Music, Cheerful Décor, Plants and a Great View*** -

Depending on the individual, such amenities can be conducive to creative and productive work.

Ideas and Information on Equipment and Supplies

Consider buying or subscribing, at least temporarily, to one or more of the following magazines:

- *Home Office Computing*, monthly magazine.

  Address:
  Home Office Computing
  156 West 56th St.
  New York, NY 10019

  http://www.smalloffice.com/
  Tel: 1-800-288-7812

  Note: A free weekly email newsletter is available through the website.

- *Small Business Computing and Communications*, monthly magazine.

  Address:
  Small Business Computing and Communications Magazine
  P. O. Box 59902
  Boulder, CO 80322-9902

  http://www.smalloffice.com/
  Tel: 1-800-537-4368

It's All Ephemeral

Think ahead a few months to a few years, especially from a cash flow and net income perspective. The supplies you buy will have to be replaced. More importantly, the much more costly equipment that you buy will need to be replaced. While computers and printers may function for many years, their useful life to you will probably be only several years because of the rapidly changing nature of technology. Be prepared to spend – spend – spend on supplies and equipment. And as you spend, be thankful for the following:

- With each subsequent computer and related equipment purchase, you will get more performance for your money.
- Because of the availability of computer and related equipment, and continuous improvements in that equipment, you can be a sole proprietor. You can be a viable player and compete on a level playing field with the "big boys and girls."

MAKING IT LEGAL: SELECTING A FORM OF OWNERSHIP

You will have to decide, primarily for income tax purposes, on the form of business ownership you will use. This decision should be made when you start your business, so you know what kind of records to keep. However, you may be able to wait awhile, but you must decide before preparing your first set of income tax forms.

The three broad options for the form of ownership are the sole proprietorship, the partnership, and the corporation. Although each of these options are briefly discussed here, the sole proprietorship is probably the most logical initial form of business ownership for you. The following discussion of these three forms of business ownership is based on Clough (1986, Chapter 2), Martin (1993, pp. 172-174), Morton (1983), Roemer (1989), and Stephens (1993).

Sole Proprietorship

With the sole proprietorship, an individual owns and operates the business. The advantage of the sole proprietorship is that it is the simplest and least expensive to establish and operate. An example of simplicity is that U.S. income tax reporting consists of completing one tax schedule for inclusion with the proprietor's personal tax return. That form is Schedule C, Profit or Loss From Business. Furthermore, there is maximum freedom of action in that the sole proprietor is the "boss" and can act unilaterally in all decisions. The most significant negative aspect of the sole proprietorship is that the owner is personally liable, including his or her personal—that is, nonbusiness—assets, for all debts and obligations. In addition, the size of the business and the ability to expand are limited by the sole proprietor's resources or his or her ability to obtain financing.

Partnership

In a partnership, two or more persons own and operate the business, although ownership, decision-making, debts, losses, and profits are not necessarily equally shared. Partnerships are formed and operated under state partnership laws. The laws generally recognize the partnership as an entity separate from the individual partners. For example, partners pay income taxes, not the partnership. Any partner can act on behalf of the partnership, provided the action is in keeping with the scope of the business.

The appeal of a partnership is that it combines the financial assets and talents of two or more individuals who are interested in engaging in the same type of business. On the negative side, particularly when compared to a sole proprietorship, individual partners are restricted in their business actions, but typically have much more latitude than owners of a corporation. For example, a partner cannot sell or mortgage his or her share of the partnership's assets without permission of the other partners. Furthermore, in a fashion similar to the sole proprietorship, each partner is financially responsible for the acts of all the partners in the full extent of his or her personal assets.

Corporation

A corporation is an entity created under state incorporation laws, consisting of one or more individuals, owned by one or more stockholders, and considered to be separate from the employees or the owners. A board of directors, elected by the owners, provides general control. The corporation can buy and sell real estate property, enter into agreements, and sue and be sued. A corporation can be dissolved by surrender or expiration of its state charter with its business obligations settled in accordance with those laws. Owners pay taxes only on dividends received after the corporation pays state and federal taxes. An S corporation is a special U.S. form of corporation available to businesses that have 35 or fewer shareholders and meet other requirements. The advantage of this form of corporation is that it has less tax liability than a standard corporation.

A significant advantage of a corporation, contrasted with a sole proprietorship or a partnership, is the limited liability of the owners. Stockholder liability is limited, with a few exceptions, to the amount of their investment in the corporation. Examples of exceptions, that is, situations in which one or more individuals within a corporation risk personal liability, are when fraud is committed or when a corporation is underfunded or underinsured. Other advantages of corporations are the ability to raise large amounts of capital and the corporation's perpetual organizational life, that is, continuation of the organization is not dependent on particular employees or owners, because the corporation is an entity separate from the employees and owners.

Another advantage of a corporation is that it provides ease of multiple ownership.

A possible disadvantage of a corporation is that the stockholders are not in any way agents of the corporation. The board of directors controls the corporation, and the officers of the board act as agents for the corporation. Stated differently, although each stockholder owns a part of the organization, he or she cannot act unilaterally on behalf of the organization.

Closure

From a legal perspective, three forms of business ownership are available to you. The sole proprietorship is probably the best choice, at least for the start up of your individual practice.

WHAT'S IN A NAME? NAMING YOUR SOLE PROPRIETORSHIP

Your parents probably gave considerable thought to selecting your name. Those of us who are parents probably did the same for our children. Similarly, you should carefully select the name of your sole proprietorship. That is, what will appear on your business cards, stationary, marketing materials and in business directories, and possibly in the Yellow Pages? Some factors to consider are:

1. Your name and the reputation you've earned under that "label" might be one of your greatest intangible assets. Therefore, consider using your name as your business' name. Your business card, for a sole proprietorship, might read:

   Mary S. Tompkins, P.E., Consultant.

Perhaps you want to more precisely define the services you offer. In that case, consider a name like:

Mary S. Tompkins, P.E., Structural Design.

2. If you plan to quickly grow from a sole proprietorship to a business with employees, you may want to start out with a flexible name like:

   Mary S. Tompkins & Associates
   or
   Tompkins Associates.

   This approach capitalizes on the well-earned reputation of your name while leaving open the growth door.

3. Another tactic is to select a non-personal name that creatively suggests what you and/or your firm will eventually do. This approach is illustrated by the following actual names of service firms:

   - Earth Tech
   - Corporate Media Group
   - Creative Computing
   - youachieve.com

In a related matter, consider developing a very short—one sentence or less—description of your services. This has many uses. It could appear on your business cards, stationary and marketing materials and could be your concise answer to the question: So what do you do? Examples of actual "one liners" (the last five are from Handy, 1998, p. 71) are:

- "From the top down, management consulting services for underground projects." (Brierly Associates)

- "The comfort of home while you're away from home." (Description of Business Class rooms at Ramada Limited/Inns/Plaza)
- "Delivering business benefits through technology." (TSC, Technical Solutions Company)
- "Helping individuals and organizations engineer their futures." (S. G. Walesh, Consultant)
- "To preserve and improve human life." (Merck)
- "To experience the joy of advancing and applying technology for the benefit of the public." (Sony)
- "To give unlimited opportunity to women." (Mary Kay Cosmetics)
- "To give ordinary folk the chance to buy the same things as rich people." (Wal-Mart)
- "To make people happy." (Walt Disney)

SOMETHING'S MISSING

As stated at its beginning, this chapter is based on the assumption that you have, or soon will have, a consulting assignment. Is that true? If not, move on to Chapter 7, "Marketing: Sleazy Activity or Mutually-Beneficial Process?"

REVIEW

In summary, let's review the main points in this chapter titled "Logistics of Getting Started." Whether your office should be inside or outside of your home is likely to depend on four factors. They are cost, professional impression, conflict with home life, and legal considerations. In addition to traditional office equipment and supplies, effective functioning in today's fast-paced marketplace requires an array of electronic devices. You are very likely to need a computer, a printer, a fax machine, and a wireless telephone. From a legal perspective, three forms of business ownership are available to you. They are the sole proprietorship, the partnership and the corporation. The best choice for you, at least at the beginning, is probably the sole proprietorship. In naming your free lance business, consider capitalizing on your name, that is, your reputation. Other naming options are to select a non-personal name that indicates the type of services provided and to choose a name that would allow you to grow beyond a sole proprietorship. Finally, formulate a short, catchy, informative description of what you do and consider placing it on your business card, stationary, and other materials.

A final thought from Richard Cushing:

Plan ahead: It wasn't raining when Noah built the ark.

Chapter 7

Marketing: Sleazy Activity or Mutually Beneficial Process?

Earn trust, learn needs, close sale.
(S. G. Walesh)

YOUR ATTITUDE TOWARD MARKETING

The expression "marketing services" often engenders negative reactions or connotations. Images of brash, high-pressure car salespeople may come to the mind of the potential sole practitioner. You may be repulsed by the thought of "wasting" your professional education by doing "sales" work or even being on the receiving end of any aspect of marketing. Nevertheless, hopefully you will be at least receptive to the particular marketing model presented in this chapter. ***To the extent you learn to view marketing as earning trust and meeting client needs, which is the essence of the model offered here, you may conclude that not***

only is it an ethical process, but also a very satisfying and mutually beneficial one.

The marketing of engineered products is not explicitly treated in this chapter. However, many of the underlying principles as well as the tools and techniques are directly applicable to the marketing of engineered products. In fact, many of the principles, tools and techniques set forth in this chapter are applicable to marketing efforts in non-business areas.

THE FINANCIAL MOTIVATION FOR CAREFULLY MANAGING MARKETING

Income for an individual practitioner emanates from one source: clients who need and are willing to pay for services. Marketing is a major expense for the sole proprietor—it consumes valuable hours and dollars. Therefore, the marketing effort must be carefully managed. As suggested by FIGURE 7-1, you should plan and implement a continuous, proactive marketing process, not a series of sporadic reactions "when you need work."

DEFINITIONS OF MARKETING AND SOME OBSERVATIONS

According to Cronk, "Marketing is creating the climate that will bring in future business" (Cronk quoted by Smallowitz and Molyneux, 1987). Kotler and Fox (1985, p. xiii) state that "Marketing is the effective management by an institution of its exchange relations with its various markets and publics."

According to W. Coxe "Marketing is to selling as fishing is to catching" (Coxe quoted by Smallowitz and Molyneux, 1987). This definition, which is illustrated in FIGURE 7-2 and FIGURE 7-3, suggests that making the sale, that is, selling is only one small

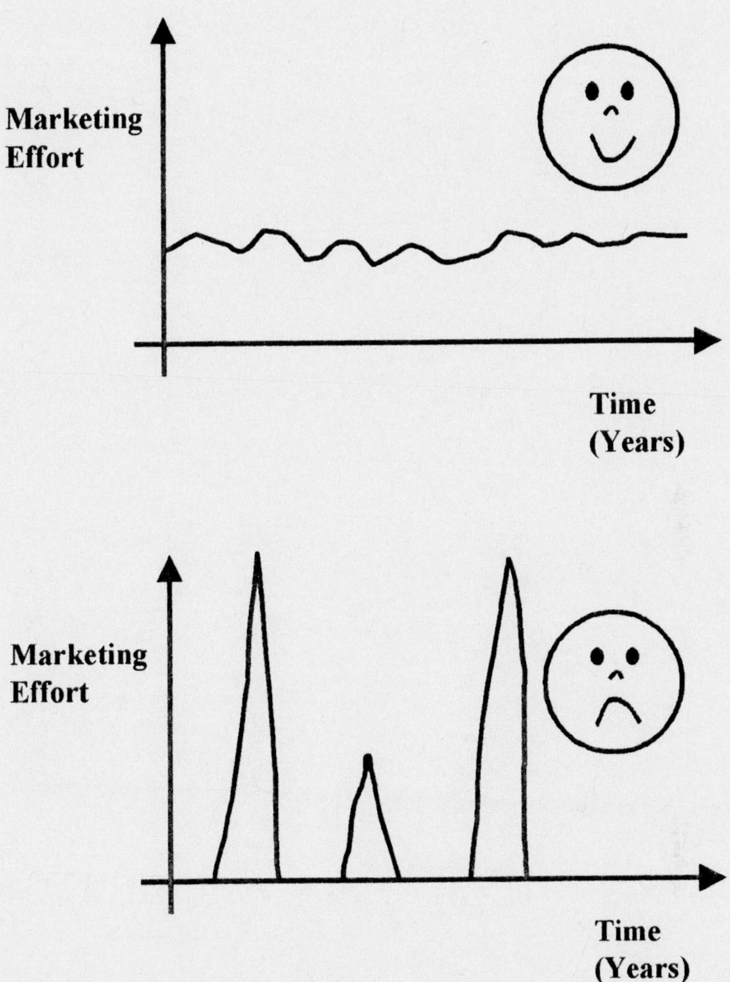

Figure 7-1. Marketing should be a continuous, proactive process and not a series of sporadic reactions.

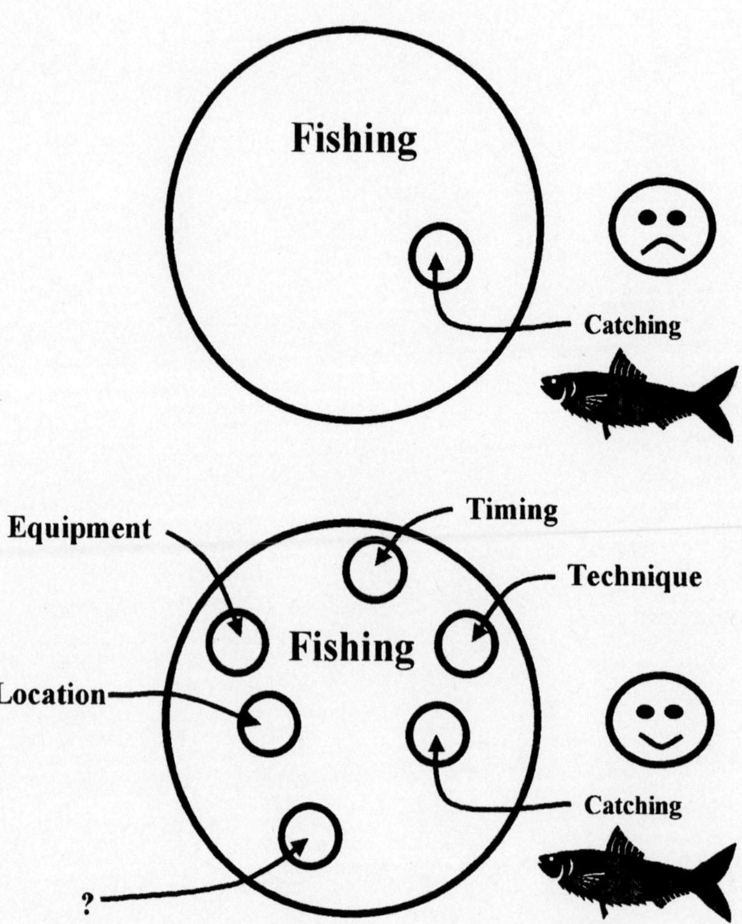

Figure 7-2. Catching is only one part of fishing.

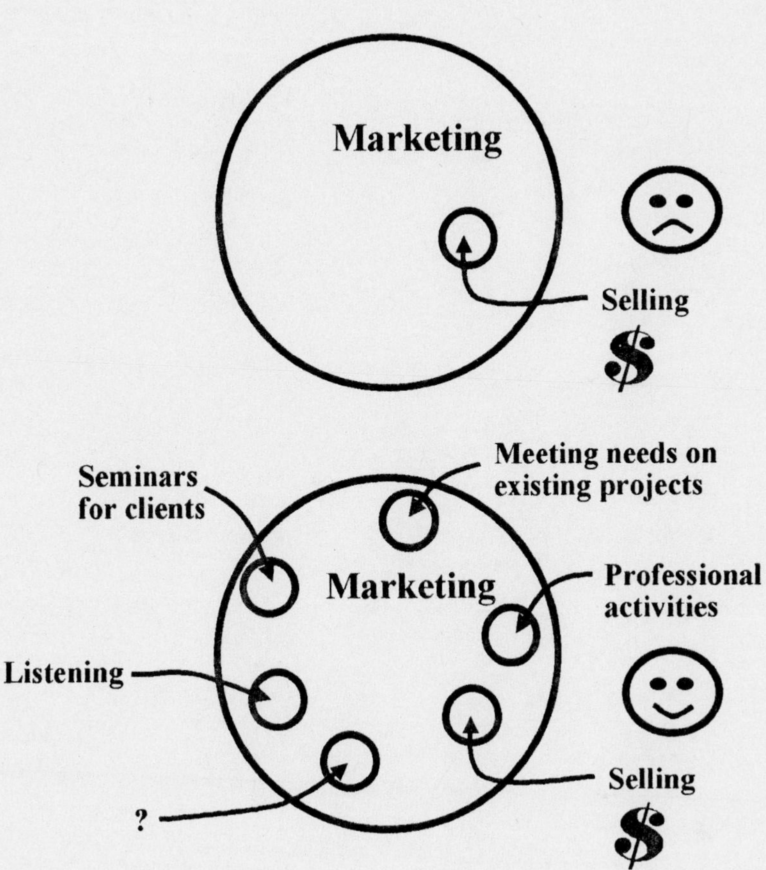

Figure 7-3. Marketing is to selling as fishing is to catching.

aspect of marketing. Similarly, catching fish is only one small part of the overall fishing process. This definition further suggests that an individual or organization must undertake a range of activities under the general umbrella of marketing in order to achieve sales. Similarly, one must carry out certain activities using specialized equipment under the general umbrella of fishing in order to actually catch fish. Or stated differently, if an individual or organization attempts to simply sell without seeing selling in the context of other activities, the individual or organization is likely to be unsuccessful. Similarly, if one seeks to catch fish without doing the related activities and using proper equipment, one is not likely to be successful.

Drucker succinctly states that "The aim of marketing is to make selling superfluous" (Drucker quoted by Kotler and Fox, 1985, p. 7). This definition, like the previous one, reinforces the idea that selling is only one part of marketing and suggests that if marketing is done well, sales will occur naturally. Some characteristics of marketing that follow from or are consistent with the preceding definitions, based in part on Kotler and Fox (1985, pp. 7-8), are:

- Marketing is much more than selling.
- Marketing is a managed process, not a collection of random actions. It involves analysis, planning, implementation, and control.
- Marketing involves mutually beneficial exchanges of needs and services or products.

MARKETING RESEARCH

The literature contains the results of some marketing or related studies that help interpret the relevance of and the desired approach to marketing of products and services. For example,

System Corporation studied 3,000 industrial salespeople in about 1988. This study, which included ratings by the customers of the sales representatives, concluded that "The ability to establish trust" was more important than likeability (Sheridan, 1988.) Rabeler (1991) cites references that, like the System Corporation study, emphasize the prime role of trust in marketing. The focus on trust in the cited studies is noteworthy and is discussed again later in this chapter.

Hensey (1987) conducted a study in 1986 of 25 of the most profitable U.S. consulting engineering firms. One significant finding for the most profitable firms was that the average percentage of repeat work for clients was 90% compared to 60% for all firms nationwide. Results of this study are consistent with experience which suggests the impact of repeat work on profitability and suggests that high levels of repeat work and profitability are achieved by ***caring for current clients***. This is a crucial concept for the individual practitioner.

Wahby (1993) effectively communicates the importance of giving attention to and taking care of existing clients when he says, "The best firms understand that ***if a project is an apple, a client is an apple tree***." This concept is illustrated in FIGURE 7-4. According to Wahby, appreciative firms "...spend the bulk of their marketing efforts judiciously cultivating, pruning, and harvesting their 'orchard' of past and current clients."

One way to test the intensity of your focus on clients is to think through how you would prepare for a meeting with a prospective client. Would you be in a "telling" mode or an "asking" mode? As suggested by FIGURE 7-5, the asking mode is preferable. We learn very little while we are talking. Maybe there's a reason we have two ears and one mouth.

Figure 7-4. If a project is an apple, a client is an apple tree.

List of Things to Tell Client:

I DON'T CARE HOW MUCH YOU KNOW UNTIL I KNOW HOW MUCH YOU CARE

List of Things to Ask Client:

Figure 7-5. Preparing for a meeting with a potential client.

> *One of the best ways to persuade others is with your ears—by listening to them.* (Dean Rusk, 1909-97)

The preceding argument for listening is that it helps the listener. That is, by talking less and listening more, you are much more likely to obtain ideas and information to support your marketing efforts.

Listening also helps the speaker. Being listened to, more specifically, being actively listened to, helps the speaker organize and articulate ideas, thoughts, concerns and expectations. The benefit to the speaker can go beyond clarification. As observed by Peck (1997, p. 51) "...the knowledge that one is being truly listened to is frequently, in and of itself, remarkably therapeutic."

Concluding Observations

Marketing research and case studies, like those presented here, suggest that you, operating as a free lancer, will be successful in marketing if you:

- Earn the trust of potential clients
- Know and focus on your strengths
- Peer into the future and proactively prepare for it with an on-going marketing effort—rather than sporadically reacting.
- Appreciate and take care of existing clients

SUGGESTED WORKING MODEL FOR PLANNING AND IMPLEMENTING A MARKETING PROGRAM

Concepts

Covey (1990, pp. 255-257) notes that the Greek philosophy for what might now be called win/win interpersonal and inter-organizational relations was based on ethos, pathos, and logos. According to Covey:

- "Ethos is your personal credibility, the faith people have in your integrity and competency. It's the trust that you inspire...."
- "Pathos is the empathic side—it's the feeling. It means you are in alignment with the emotional thrust of another's communication."
- "Logos is the logic, the reasoning part of the presentation."

Covey emphasizes that these three elements of win/win interpersonal and inter-organizational relations must occur in the indicated order. That is, trust must be established first, then needs must be understood, and then a logical follow-up occurs.

Applicability to Marketing

The ethos-pathos-logos sequence can serve as a positive, very effective marketing model. The ethos-pathos-logos view of marketing as a mutually beneficial process is illustrated in FIGURE 7-6. To reiterate, the indicated sequence must be followed. The rational tendency in interpersonal relations, however, is to start with logos which usually leads to less than satisfactory results. Engineers and other technical professionals may be inclined to proceed too quickly and rely too heavily on logic.

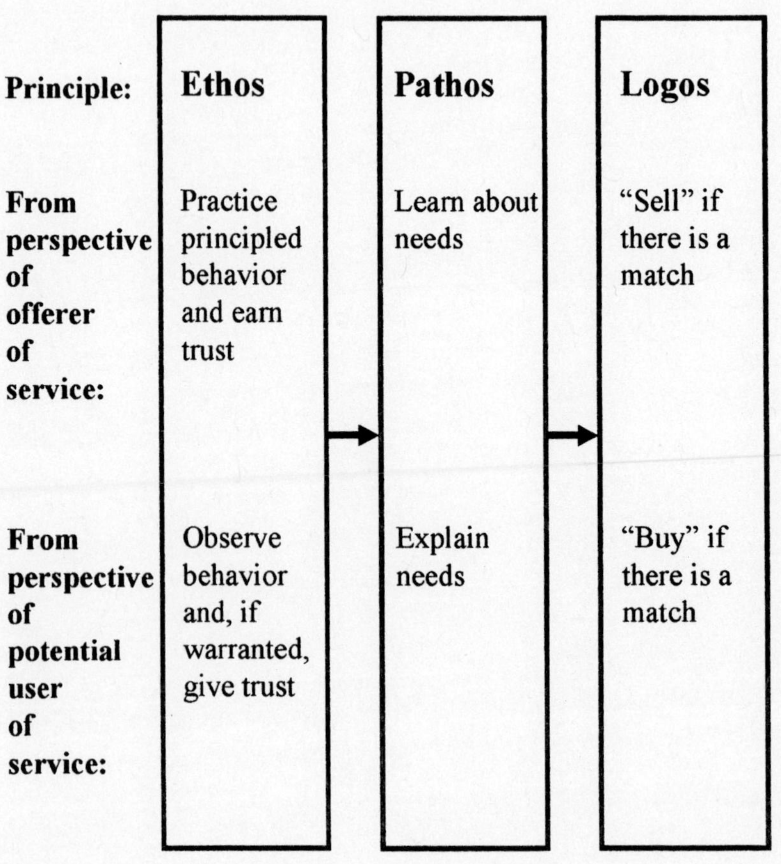

Figure 7-6. The ethos-pathos-logos view of marketing.

The point of all of this is that the sequential ethos-pathos-logos process is an excellent basis for marketing. That is, first establish trust, then understand needs, and then follow-up logically. You, as an individual practitioner, must first earn the trust of potential clients. Once that trust is established, potential clients are likely to reveal their needs to you. If there is a match, that is, if you can meet those needs, then a logical follow-up in the form of a contract or agreement is likely to occur.

If a match does not develop between you and the potential client, then you should provide assistance by referring the potential client to another individual or organization. Remember, your first goal is to earn trust. Being truly helpful, by making a thoughtful referral, is one way to do that.

To reiterate, an excellent foundation for your individual marketing effort is:

- Ethos - earn trust
- Pathos - learn needs
- Logos - close deal

TOOLS AND TECHNIQUES

Many specific tools and techniques are available for implementing a marketing program. An effective set of tools and techniques must be selected for each of the three steps, that is, earning trust, learning needs and closing the deal. Some available tools and techniques are summarized in FIGURE 7-7, where they appear as rows. The three steps in the marketing process correspond to the three right columns.

A sole proprietor could use this matrix, or a variation on it, to prepare a detailed marketing plan and then to implement the plan. The effort would, of course, be tailored to the individual practitioner's situation. Although he or she should use all three

Figure 7-7. Marketing tools and techniques can be chosen to implement the three-step marketing model. (1 of 8)

Marketing Tools and Techniques	Marketing Steps			
Name	Reference	Earn Trust	Learn Needs	Close Deal
Conduct of internal meeting, workshop, or retreat to define strengths.			●	
Assessment of recent fees by service type, clients, geographic area.	Dupies, 1979		●	
Assessment of marketing costs-relative to total fees and fees by service area.	Dupies, 1979		●	
Analysis of demographic and economic data.	Dupies, 1979		●	
Analysis of existing and pending local, state, and federal laws and regulations.	Dupies, 1979		●	
Interviews/surveys of clients and community leaders with emphasis on services needed and how the service firm is viewed.	Dupies, 1979	●	●	

Figure 7-7. Marketing tools and techniques can be chosen to implement the three-step marketing model. (2 of 8)

Marketing Tools and Techniques		Marketing Steps		
Name	Reference	Earn Trust	Learn Needs	Close Deal
Emphasis on benefits, not features.	Dehne,1991	●		
	Heightchew, 1999			
Hiring personnel predisposed to marketing.	Talbot, 1998	●	●	
Advertising.	Competitive Advantage, 1988	●		
	Groob et al., 1987			
Audiovisuals.	Groob et al., 1987	●		
Brochures.	Groob et al., 1987	●		
Creative use of voicemail.	Benun	●	●	
Interviewing lost clients.		●	●	
Learning about a potential client's policies, practices and personnel.	Avila, 1995	●	●	

Figure 7-7. Marketing tools and techniques can be chosen to implement the three-step marketing model. (3 of 8)

Marketing Tools and Techniques	Marketing Steps			
Name	Reference	Earn Trust	Learn Needs	Close Deal
Direct mail.	Benun	●	●	
	Competitive Advantage, 1988			
	Devonshire Financial, 1988			
	Groob et al., 1987			
Email (broadcast via internet)	Benun, 2000	●	●	
Trade show displays.	Devonshire Financial, 1988	●	●	
	Groob et al., 1987			
Statement of qualifications.	Groob et al., 1987	●		
Newsletter (mailed) with response mechanism.	Groob et al., 1987	●	●	

Figure 7-7. Marketing tools and techniques can be chosen to implement the three-step marketing model. (4 of 8)

Marketing Tools and Techniques	Marketing Steps			
Name	Reference	Earn Trust	Learn Needs	Close Deal
Newsletter (broadcast via internet) with invitation to respond.		●	●	
Listing in professional directories.	Snyder, 1993, p. 29	●		
Website.	Lantos, 1998	●	●	
Press releases.	Benun	●		
	Groob et al., 1987			
	O'Connor, 1999	●	●	
Participating in joint ventures.	Snyder, 1993, p. 31	●	●	
Using office to make desired impression.	Competitive Advantage, 1988	●		
Asking existing clients to call potential clients.		●		
Entering projects in award competition.		●		
Sending business leads to private-sector potential clients.		●		

Figure 7-7. Marketing tools and techniques can be chosen to implement the three-step marketing model. (5 of 8)

Marketing Tools and Techniques	Marketing Steps			
Name	Reference	Earn Trust	Learn Needs	Close Deal
Sending articles published by others.	Isphording, 1990	●		
Distributing copies of papers published/ presented by firm's personnel.		●		
Calling "your" office anonymously or asking a friend to visit "your" office.	Groob et al., 1987 Townsend, 1970, p. 31.	●		
Entertaining clients/potential clients.	Isphording, 1990	●	●	
Sending a prospecting letter or email to targeted clients/potential clients.	Lantos, 1998	●	●	
Presenting/publishing papers.	Lantos, 1998	●	●	
Writing column for a professional organization's newsletter or for a newspaper.	Schillaci, 1995	●	●	

Figure 7-7. Marketing tools and techniques can be chosen to implement the three-step marketing model. (6 of 8)

Marketing Tools and Techniques	Marketing Steps			
Name	Reference	Earn Trust	Learn Needs	Close Deal
Conducting seminars for clients/potential clients.	Holtz, 1987 Isphording, 1990 Severn et al., 1994	●	●	
Writing and distributing white papers on timely topics.	Hewlett-Packard, 1995	●	●	
Co-authoring papers with clients.		●	●	
Hosting client/potential client visits to firm's office.	Isphording, 1990	●	●	
Hosting client/potential client visits to firm's projects and/or clients.		●	●	
Participating actively in civic and professional organizations.	Isphording, 1990	●	●	
Visiting clients/potential clients.	Isphording, 1990 Bakan, 1985	●	●	

Figure 7-7. Marketing tools and techniques can be chosen to implement the three-step marketing model. (7 of 8)

Marketing Tools and Techniques	Marketing Steps			
Name	Reference	Earn Trust	Learn Needs	Close Deal
Asking open-ended questions.	Competitive Advantage, 1988	●	●	
Assigning backup partners/principals to each client.	Isphording, 1990	●	●	
Inviting clients/potential clients to in-house training and education events.		●	●	
Admitting mistakes and suggesting or taking remedial actions.	Rabeler, 1991	●		
Maintaining master resumes of staff members with emphasis on achievements.		●		
Recognizing achievements/milestones of clients/potential clients.	Isphording, 1990	●		
Maintaining a list of personal references.		●		

Figure 7-7. Marketing tools and techniques can be chosen to implement the three-step marketing model. (8 of 8)

Marketing Tools and Techniques		Marketing Steps		
Name	Reference	Earn Trust	Learn Needs	Close Deal
Maintaining descriptions of on-going and completed projects.		●		
Conducting completed project postmortem with client.			●	
Gathering data on client/potential client.	Bakan,1985		●	
Following up on leads.	Groob et al., 1987		●	
Asking for contract.				●
Hand delivering reports.	Rabeler, 1991	●	●	
Placing signs at the sites of on-going projects.		●		
Saying thank you to clients and project participants.		●	●	

steps (the last three columns in the matrix), and generally perform them sequentially with any given client, only the potentially most effective of the 56 listed tools and techniques (the rows) would be utilized. Note that only one of the 56 tools and techniques ("ask for contract") is "selling."

Some of the listed marketing tools and techniques such as your resume, a list of completed projects, a list of references, and SOQ should be kept on a word processing system—not in hard copy. Resist the temptation to have one resume, one list of projects, one reference list, one set of testimonials, one list of papers and presentations, and one SOQ for all purposes. Not only will this approach generally result in documents of excessive length, which will probably not be read, but it also will result in documents that are not responsive to the current and specified needs of potential clients. Respond quickly to a question or a RFP by carefully extracting sections of master materials to create special short documents tailored to specific situations.

As a way of concluding this discussion of a marketing model and supporting tools and techniques for the sole proprietor, refer to FIGURE 7-8. Presented there are ideas on marketing approaches that are likely to "work" and "not work." The overall message of FIGURE 7-8 and the theme of this chapter is that marketing can be a satisfying experience for you and your clients/potential clients if based on the "earn trust – learn needs – close deal" model.

YOUR CURRENT EMPLOYER MIGHT BE YOUR FIRST CLIENT

You are probably not leaving your current employer because he or she doesn't need you but probably because you need something else in your work life. Don't "burn any bridges" with your employer when you resign. Assuming you and your

Figure 7-8. Experience reveals "what works" and "what doesn't work" in marketing. (1 of 2)

WHAT WORKS	WHAT DOESN'T WORK
Listening—to earn trust and learn needs	Talking—about what we do
Building relationships	Pursuing projects
Asking questions	Pontificating
Researching, qualifying and ranking potential clients	Viewing clients as equals
Active involvement in targeted professional/business organizations	Passive membership in randomly selected professional/business organizations
Keeping current—technically and otherwise	Maintaining status quo
Getting leads and following up	Getting leads and expecting others to follow-up
"Face time"	Mass mailings
What you see is what you get	Bait and switch
Illustrating benefits	Pushing features
Multiple level contacts with client	Single level contact
Written materials featuring white space, graphics, photographs, color, variety	Lots of words
Suggesting program and project approaches	Reacting to RFP's
Client-oriented project descriptions, SOQ's, proposals and interviews	Consultant-oriented project descriptions, SOQ's, proposals and interviews

Figure 7-8. Experience reveals "what works" and "what doesn't work" in marketing. (2 of 2)

WHAT WORKS	WHAT DOESN'T WORK
Tailoring to client	Boilerplating from files
Defining and meeting requirements	Talking "quality" and spewing slogans
Preparing project work plans and sharing with client	"Winging it"
Delivering locally while drawing globally	Attempting to do it all locally
Admitting errors and fixing them	Blaming others
Asking clients how they want to communicate	Using firm's preferred mode of communication
Delivering draft deliverables to client throughout the project	Dumping deliverables on client at the end of the project
Caring for existing clients—performing on their projects	Neglecting existing clients—chasing new ones
"Rifle"	"Shotgun"
Making promises and delivering	Breaking promises and offering excuses
Perseverance	Instant success
Saying "thank you"	---

employer are on good terms, and that trust has been established, there may be a mutually beneficial reason for you and they to enter into an agreement. This conservative approach is in the spirit of the rule of wing walking, that is, don't let go of what you have until you have something else (Latamore, 1999).

The agreement might be as simple as an hourly rate and defined expense reimbursements if and when your former employer needs assistance. That assistance might include finishing up some projects you were working on, tutoring your replacement, marketing based on relationships you've developed, or breaking new ground. At the other end of the spectrum, the agreement might be more complex and include a retainer for you that guarantees a minimum monthly income. Perhaps you and your former employer will negotiate an exclusive arrangement whereby you are committed to serving only them in certain well-defined areas of expertise, or geographic locations.

The key thought is not to overlook the obvious. Your current employer could be your first client. Your current employer may also refer clients to you—and you may refer clients to them. After all, you know each other very well.

TRACKING MARKETING EFFORTS AND PLANNING MARKETING ACTIONS

Because you, as a sole proprietor, will be solely responsible for the logistics of your marketing program, you will need two things: One is self discipline, and lots of it; and the other is a system for monitoring what you've done and planning what you are going to do. Frequently refer to your system as a reminder of actions you need to take relative to one or more potential clients. Always have at least one action item planned for each client or potential client.

One approach to a system is to maintain a simple chronological list of past and planned actions for each client/potential client. APPENDIX 7-1 is an example. Nothing fancy—but it works!

One step beyond building your own system "from scratch" is to start with a database program such as Microsoft Access, Lotus Approach, or File Maker Pro (Bradley, 2000). Advantages of this approach are that you can custom design your system while using the software's report-generation features.

Another option, simpler but less flexible than the preceding, is to use a commercial contact management package. Examples are Act 2000 (from Symantec, http://www.symantec.com/act), Maximizer 5.0 (from Multiactive Software; http://www.maximizer.com) and Outlook 2000 (from Microsoft, http://www.microsoft.com).

You decide how to "do it," that is, use a self-developed system, a database program, or a contact management package. However "not doing it" is not an option. You must be continuously involved in proactive marketing and, to do it intelligently, you need a system. As illustrated by APPENDIX 7-1, only a small fraction of leads will result in contracts. Furthermore, several to many contacts initiated by you are typically required before a lead becomes a sale. The specific system you select is 5% of the effort, the other 95% is your commitment to use the system in doing your marketing.

Benun (1999) devotes an issue of her newsletter to the necessity of taking a disciplined structured approach to marketing and other aspects of sole proprietorships. Structured marketing tactics suggested in the newsletter include:

- Schedule one day a week to make follow up calls.
- Drop a lead only if asked to.

- Set a goal for every marketing telephone call.
- Commit to two to three monthly seminars, volunteer, or other interaction activities.
- Thank your clients for every project.
- Maintain (electronically) a variety of boilerplate marketing materials.
- Send one press release per month.

You may ask: how may I continuously market and also work productively on my client's projects? Answer: have, or develop, the self-discipline to devote, on an almost daily basis, a small percent of your time to marketing. Do this even when you are swamped with billable work. Refer again to FIGURE 7-1, which emphasizes the need to market continuously.

A possible analogous question is: how can I carry out my daily responsibilities and also grow hair on my head? Somehow, you manage. Marketing your sole proprietorship must be as on-going and automatic as growing hair on your head.

Follow the preceding proactive, on-going marketing monitoring and planning advice, and you will quickly work your way into a situation in which you will have too many business opportunities. Such a problem! Fail to act on the preceding proactive, on-going marketing advice and your individual practitioner business will die.

Remember, the sole reason you are in business is to meet client needs. Marketing is the process (earning trust, learning needs, closing sale) by which you learn about needs and position yourself to meet those needs, in a mutually beneficial manner.

PROPOSALS

Assume that the "earn trust – learn needs – close sale" process, or some variation on it, results in a potential client asking for a proposal. That is, you and a potential client agree that your mutual interests might be served by working together.

Your proposal should address, at least in a preliminary manner, issues such as your and the client's responsibilities, schedule, and cost.

The proposal might be in the form of a conversation between you and the potential client confirmed, symbolically or actually, by a handshake. Sometimes that discussion is formalized in the form of a short letter. An example of a short, informal letter proposal is included as APPENDIX 7-2.

Other times, you will be asked to prepare a more detailed, formal letter proposal. The format and content may be prescribed by the potential client or you may have the opportunity to structure it. APPENDIX 7-3 is an example of a long, formal letter proposal.

LEVERAGE YOUR MARKETING SUCCESSES

Be alert to the possibility of pro-actively leveraging efforts on one new project or series of new projects with the goal of obtaining additional assignments with existing or new clients. This can be a very cost-effective marketing tactic. As you pass the midpoint of any project, but especially one with useful new or unique concepts, methodologies, or deliverables, start to think how elements of that project might meet the needs of other clients. Besides the value you are providing to the client you are serving, how can you provide value to other existing or potential clients?

Two examples, based on actual situations, follow:

1. A sole proprietor created many and varied E&T materials as a result of leading workshops or seminars. The consultant was aware that some engineering firms are concerned that their younger engineers and other technical professionals lack business savvy. He scanned the E&T materials and assembled a list of 16 topics suitable for younger professionals. The list was presented to the manager of one office of an existing client as "The Business of Consulting: A Seminar Series for Entry Level and Other Younger Professionals." The consultant was retained, on a sole source basis, to present a series of noon hour and late afternoon-early evening workshops in that office.

   Note that both parties—the consulting firm and the individual practitioner—"win." The consulting firm obtains current E&T appropriate to the needs of the target audience and at reasonable cost because the sole proprietor did not have to prepare material "from scratch". The free lancer obtains an additional profitable assignment, exposure to more members of the firm, and another project to show on his resume.

2. While employed with a consulting firm and later as a consultant to the firm, a free lancer works on an innovative and unique technical solution to a common public works problem. Realizing that the technology may interest the R&D community and may be supportive of a federal R&D oriented agency, the consultant approaches the federal agency. Result: the individual practitioner obtains a substantial contract

with that agency to prepare a case study report on the innovative and unique project.

The preceding leveraging tactics, when viewed retrospectively, may seem obvious. However, undertaking them or similar tactics requires creativity and self-discipline, especially if you are already very busy with contracted work. Contracted project work can very easily, to your long term detriment, take total precedence over "obvious" marketing efforts.

KISS

The underlying message of this marketing chapter is that the free lancer, in doing marketing, should KISS (Keep it simple, stupid!). Simple doesn't mean easy. "All" that's needed to obtain many, varied, challenging and profitable contracts is to:

- Earn trust, learn needs, close sale: This requires persistence and patience.
- Be continuously marketing: This requires a logistical system and a high degree of self-discipline, especially when you are extremely busy with current contracts.

GO OUT ON A LIMB

A unifying theme of this chapter is the principle that marketing requires a systematic, persistent, patient approach. However, the sole proprietor should occasionally, as an exception to the rule, do something impulsive, unplanned, "risky." Go out on a limb. Take a flyer. Look over the top of your silo. Leap before you look. Take a shot in the dark. Think outside of the box.

Why? Because by doing so you are likely to discover something new and valuable (not necessarily positive) about yourself while opening doors of opportunity. You may expand your network, land a lead, or, in rare circumstances, secure a project. Frances Bacon, the English philosopher and statesman, put it this way: "A wise man will make more opportunities then he finds."

Because going out on a limb is so individual and circumstance specific, meaningful examples are difficult to present. However, for illustration purposes, consider the following, all of which are based on actual situations:

- Contact your local or regional newspaper, television or radio station. Explain that you are an expert in XYZ and are available to be of assistance to reporters. Nothing may come of your offer but, on the other hand, you may become the regional XYZ expert!

- Think of a prestigious or otherwise desirable organization that you would like to serve as a consultant or an employee. Call a decision-maker at that organization, frankly tell them of your desire to serve and why. Nothing may happen but, on the other hand, you may land an exciting new client.

- Identify a controversial issue in your field about which you have a strong, informed opinion. Submit a thought-provoking letter to the editor of a widely read journal, magazine or newspaper. Nothing may happen but, on the other hand, a series of enlightening follow-up letters may appear and you may meet some interesting and powerful people. You may be surprised with the number and variety of people who "come out of the woodwork" as a result of publication of your views.

- Pick up a magazine/newsletter/journal completely outside of your professional field. As you read it, look for articles or news items having apparent connections or overlaps to what you do or know a lot about. Contact the author/editor and note the similarities between their work and yours. Nothing may come of it but, on the other hand, you may gain new insight and expand your network.

- Contact a person in your field whom you sincerely believe is highly regarded and is powerful. Explain that you are starting out or are striving to advance and would value their advice. Depending on the physical and other circumstances, offer to "buy lunch," telephone them at their convenience, or communicate by email. Be prepared with a list of five to ten concerns you have or questions you'd like to ask. Nothing may happen but, on the other hand, you may acquire a valuable coach or even mentor.

- If you have basic teaching ability and desire, and possess a body of knowledge and experience to share, contact the continuing education/training chapter of an appropriate professional/ business/education organization and offer your services (gratis or for a fee plus expenses). Taking this one step further, or going farther out on a limb, plan, advertise, conduct and follow up on your own seminar/workshop at a hotel/conference center. Nothing may happen but, on the other hand, you may have successful seminars and make many valuable contacts. The "worst" outcome is that you and possibly others incur expenses, the event is cancelled for lack of registrants, and your name and services have been exposed to 100's or

1000's of people, many of whom are potential clients or business partners.

- Call a political or other leader in your community or state. Offer your expertise for service on a committee or board. Nothing may happen but, on the other hand, you may be asked to lead an exciting new venture.

If you are shy, remember that many professional actors share this trait. However, they have learned one important principle: "Just say the lines." You can apply this principle.

Be your sane and safe self most of the time. But, every now and then, go out on a limb; that's where the best fruit may be.

REVIEW

In closing this chapter titled "Marketing: Sleazy Activity or Mutually Beneficial Process," reflect on the principal ideas offered. Marketing is essential to your success, you are totally in charge of it, and you are urged to view marketing as a satisfying and mutually beneficial process. A simple and effective marketing model can be expressed in six words: earn trust, learn needs, close sale. While the model is simple, its implementation requires persistence and patience. A long list of marketing tools and techniques is available for use within this simple model. You can choose from this list to create a marketing program suited to the needs of your sole proprietorship. Before stepping out on your own, determine if your current employer might be your first client. Your current employer may also refer clients to you and you may refer clients to them. All of this assumes that you and your employer part without "burning bridges." Develop and frequently use a system for tracking completed marketing efforts and for determining your next marketing action items.

Market continuously and leverage marketing successes. Finally, every now and then, go out on a limb.

Consider this closing thought from an unknown source:

I don't care how much you know
until I know how much you care.

Appendix 7-1. Marketing Action Items

The following is a modified and shortened version of an actual list used by a sole proprietor.

PROFESSIONAL ASSOCIATION 1

Sent memo on CD-ROM, Internet and distance learning (12/97)

"**MANAGEMENT & LEADERSHIP" SEMINAR CONDUCTED IN DENVER** (10/97)

Discussed future seminars, including distance learning with CJ (10/5/97)

Presented distance learning experiment idea to CJ and RL (10/97)

Sent email to CJ suggesting another R3 seminar based on Denver success (10/26/97)

Talked to CJ, looking for ideas including those related to distance learning, sent info (2/98)

Two seminars scheduled for early 1999

Telephone contact with WJ who is in charge of "in-house" offerings. He mentioned Seattle firm and PM seminar potential (11/98).

Milwaukee firm PM seminar potential (11/98)

Sent info to WJ (11/98)

WJ referred me to Seattle firm. I followed up with info and then long conference call. (11/17/98)

Told WJ they were impressed with me and would make some decisions in early '99 (12/98).

SEMINARS CONDUCTED IN PHILADELPHIA

CJ and I are interested in specially recorded audio version of seminars (1/99)

CONSULTING FIRM 1

CONDUCTED 2 CAREER DEVELOPMENT SEMINARS (97)

Suggested "Business of consulting" seminar to EL (9/97)

FACILITATED STRATEGIC PLAN-OPERATING PLAN MEETING (11/97)

CONDUCTED MENTORING SEMINAR (1/98)

Business of Consulting topic arose at 11/98 planning meeting.

Sent update on some projects I am doing to BR (1/98).

Sent A5 idea to CT after discussing it earlier with him. (2/9/98)

Sent CU paper to EL and CT (3/98)

Asked BR again about "business" course when I sent first draft of mentoring handout (6/98). No response.

Sent "organizational health" draft paper to BR with suggestion that they try some of the group applications (7/1/98). No response.

Briefly discussed "Business of ..." and "Career" with BR and Sent "Business of ..." outline (8/14/98). No response.

EL asked me to conduct mentoring seminar (11/98)

CONDUCTED MENTORING SEMINAR (1/99)

Met with CT, positive, open to "Business of" (12/7/98)

Sent unsolicited proposal for "Business of," suggested repeat of career development seminars in '99, suggested "CU" (1/99)

NEXT STEP: TALK TO CT ABOUT PROPOSAL.

FEDERAL AGENCY 1

Received letter from CT, former student (6/97)
Send materials and outlined approach (7/97)
Wrote to inquire about status (12/97)
Talked to LC, on 7/24/97; reorganizing, may get back to me.
NEXT STEP: CALL LC AND SUGGEST A ONE-DAY MKT. FUNDAMENTALS SEMINAR FOR LUMP SUM

CONSULTING FIRM 2

In response to request, sent bio and other info to LB (8/27/98)
We talked and may do "trial balloon" on an acquisition—he will call (9/14/98)
We talked at NSPE meeting—he may get out of it. We discussed Germany and he mentioned a lead (11/98).
I faxed an article and asked for more info on lead (11/98)
NEXT STEP: SEND ARTICLE IDEA

CONSULTING FIRM 3

Renewed contact with HT at ACEC meeting (11/98)
Sent info and promised to call him (11/98).
Called TH and offered to drop in, no response (1/99)
NEXT STEP: TRY AGAIN NEXT TIME I WILL BE IN AREA.

SOLE PROPRIETOR 1

Sent summary of services to DR (7/95).
Sent UM flyer (3/97)
Sent NSPE 10/97 brochure plus list of

seminar/workshops (9/97)
Brought DR into FEMA street project (98)
DR briefed me on old ACME Engineers and referred me to DE (12/98)
I left message with DE (12/98)

PROFESSIONAL ASSOCIATION 2

Discussion with HR (4/95).
HR said still under consideration (5/95).
Presented talk to local chapter (10/95)
Declined to do seminar in fall '96 (7/96). Maybe in spring.
HR asked for a proposal for a one day, two topic workshop (12/97)
Submitted proposal to HR (1/98)
PRESENTED "RETROFIT" HALF OF SEMINAR (7/98)
HR asked for "non-technical" ideas
NEXT STEP: SEND IDEAS

CONSULTING FIRM 4

Received call from RO, HR Dir., formerly HR Director at CHM (4/98)
Tel call with RO, need assistance with "Education Center" (4/13/98).
Communication with SB, principal in charge (4/98)
CONSULTED WITH FIRM AND REVIEWED PROPOSED CENTER FOR EDUCATION (5/98)
SB asked me to be involved with review of firm's PM manual
I called and inquired about PM manual (6/26/98 and 7/14/98)

SB called on 7/15/98, no help needed now on Center, will recommend that I review PM manual.

Called SB's office, left message, I'm concerned, problem? (12/3/98)

SB says no problem (12/98)

Appendix 7-2. Example of a Short, Informal Letter Proposal

(Date)

(Address)

(Salutation)

This is the promised follow-up to our (DATE) discussion in your office. The purpose of this letter is to formalize our earlier discussions regarding my services to (ORGANIZATION'S NAME).

I am assisting in planning for the first annual national meeting of your firm's Water Resources service line. This effort began on (DATE) with preparation of agenda and arrangement suggestions. I will also help facilitate the meeting and prepare for and present ideas and information titled "What Clients Want." Finally, I will provide you with a post-meeting memorandum that will supplement documentation produced before and during the meeting.

My compensation is $____/hour plus expenses and I will submit detailed monthly invoices beginning in early (MONTH).

I trust the preceding is an accurate summary of my earlier service discussions with you. If so, please sign one copy of this letter and return it to me. Please let me know if you have any questions or concerns.

I appreciate this opportunity to be of service and look forward to continuing to work with you and your staff on the annual meeting, and perhaps other projects.

Sincerely,

I. Noitall
Consultant

Accepted by:

____
(Name of authorized client representative)
(Name of organization)

> (Note: This letter assumes the consultant has been selected and, in this case, the work has already begun based on an earlier verbal authorization. The letter documents what has happened and is going to happen.)

Appendix 7-3. Example of a Long, Formal Letter Proposal

(Date)

(Address)

RE: Proposal for (Name of project)

(Salutation)

This letter is in response to your request and is a follow-up to our (Date) discussion. Thank you for the opportunity to submit this proposal.

As I understand, your needs (or the key issues) are:

- ???
- ???
- ???
- ???

(Note: Indicate your understanding of what the potential client wants and/or needs or what the basic issues are. Assuming you've carefully researched the situation, including asking many and varied questions, this is where you can separate yourself from others by demonstrating that you understand the client and his/her situation.)

SCOPE OF SERVICES (or APPROACH, TASKS, etc.)

Based on my understanding of your needs (the issues), I propose to do the following:

1. Meet ......
2. Draft .....
3. Design .....
4. Prepare .....
5. Present .....
6. ???

(Note: Use the same format for all steps/tasks. For example, in the preceding list, each step/task begins with a verb.)

(Note: The purpose of the Scope of Services is to explain what you are going to do. This helps to confirm that you understand the client's wants/needs/issues. The scope also forms the basis for your labor and expense estimate.)

(Note: For each or some steps/tasks, you might indicate the results/deliverables. Clients are naturally more concerned with what they will get than what you will be doing to produce it.)

SCHEDULE

I've developed a detailed project schedule consistent with your timetable. Milestones are:

- _______, ______, 2000: Complete meetings with ______.
- _______, ______, 2000: Send draft of ____ to ______.
- _______, ______, 2000: Assist you in making a formal presentation to _______.
- _______, ______, 2000: Submit plans and specifications to _______.

> (Note: For planning purposes, you should develop a detailed schedule. Select key client-related items from that schedule and list them here.)

PROJECT MANAGEMENT (or COORDINATION, COMMUNICATION, etc.)

> (Note: Once again use what you have learned about the client, in this case how he/she prefers to work with consultants.)

I will be the principal liaison person on this project.

All work (90% of the work, etc.) will be performed by me.

As I understand, Mr./Ms. _______ will be the principal representative of your organization (firm, company, agency).

Routine communication will be by telephone (email, fax, weekly conference calls, weekly meetings in your office, etc.)

I will provide written monthly (weekly, quarterly, etc.) progress reports.

Etc.

FEE

The estimated fee (labor and expenses) for the services described above is $____. Labor will be billed at $_____/hour and expenses billed at cost. Invoices will be sent monthly (quarterly, etc.).

Or

The lump sum fee for the services described above is $_________. Invoices will be sent monthly (bimonthly, etc.) based on estimated percent complete.

> (Note: Regardless of which form of compensation is used, the understanding is that if you are asked to do more than described in the Scope of Services, additional compensation will be negotiated.)

I will regard receipt of a signed copy of this letter agreement as your authorization to proceed with the services as described above.

> (Note: The purpose of the following signoff section is to facilitate converting this letter proposal to an agreement, providing the potential client finds all aspects of the proposal acceptable.)

Please contact me if you have any questions or concerns.

Sincerely,	Accepted by:
____________________	____________________
I. Noitall	(Name of authorized client representative)
Consultant	(Name of Organization)
____________________	____________________
Date	Date

(Note: This suggested format assumes that your credentials have been established and accepted. If that is not the case, then add a section titled "QUALIFICATIONS" (or "EXPERIENCE," etc.), and possibly have attachments that further elaborate on your qualifications. Also consider a section titled "REFERENCES" that list personal references with telephone numbers, etc., or refers to an attachment that provides such information.)

Chapter 8

Tips on Being Successful With a New Client

The lure of the distant and the difficult is deceptive. The great opportunity is where you are. (John Burroughs)

A MULTI-YEAR OPPORTUNITY

Your marketing efforts have borne fruit and, hopefully, have been a satisfying experience. You and your new and perhaps first client have voluntarily come together for at least an initial assignment for one reason: mutual benefit. The client wants to obtain advice, get a solution to a problem, save money, make more profit, etc. You want to earn, learn, and make good things happen.

If, and that's a big "IF," the first assignment is mutually beneficial, it could lead to many, varied, non-competitive mutually beneficial assignments over a period of years. As an example, the author's first assignment with one client was to conduct a leadership workshop. In the subsequent six years, that client alone retained the author for over 30 additional, highly varied projects. The process is illustrated in FIGURE 8-1. Whether or not a similar growth phenomenon occurs for you will depend primarily on you—not solely on you, but primarily on you.

Incidentally, during or after the first assignment with a new client, you may decide to end the relationship even though the client may want to continue. Possible reasons include:

- Client incessantly "creeps" the scope, that is, expects you do more but not pay you more.
- Work is boring
- Work is too difficult, you are "out of your league."
- Client doesn't pay promptly and/or otherwise hassles you.
- Ethical conflicts

The preceding not withstanding, in most cases, you will want this first assignment to lead to more assignments. Three tactics are described in this chapter. A discussion of some ways in which client relationships end concludes the chapter.

BE PREPARED FOR SUSPICION AND ANIMOSITY

Your arrival may not be viewed positively. Possible reasons include:

- Personnel are insulted by the need to "bring in an outsider to do their jobs."

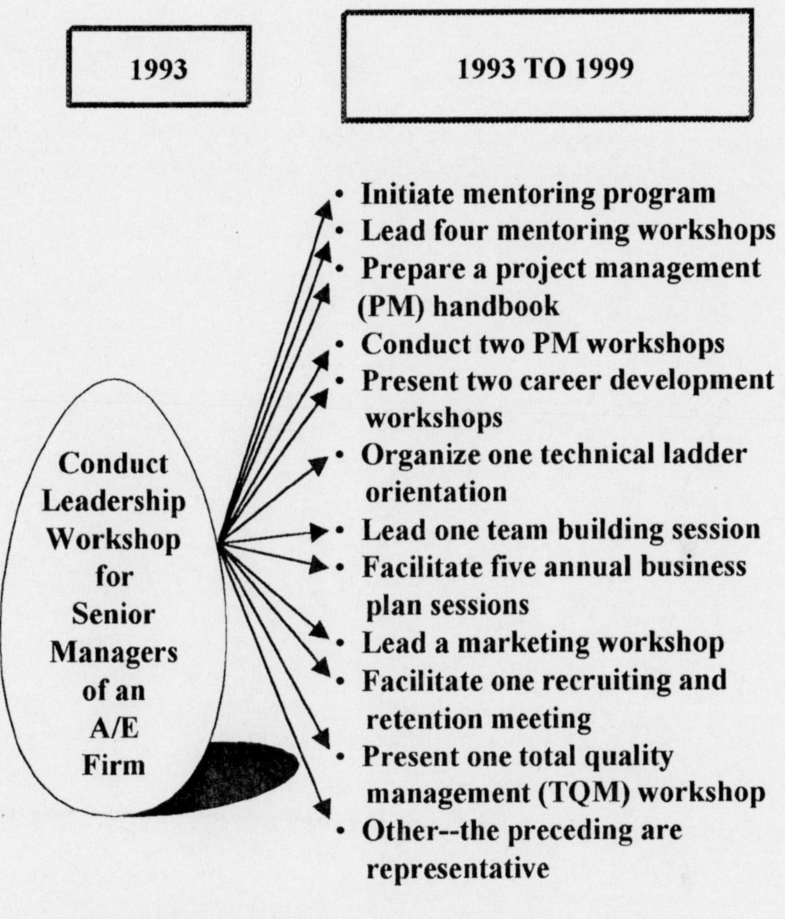

Note: The example applies to S. G. Walesh, Consultant

Figure 8-1. Mutually beneficial performance on the first assignment can lead to many assignments over many years.

- Substandard performers fear being officially identified.
- "Skeletons" may be found.
- Staff are already extremely busy and now they have to invest time in you.
- Your arrival signals the start of another "hot management fad" for which, in their opinion, much energy will be expended but there will be no follow through.

Prepare to respond to suspicion and animosity by being certain that you understand your assignment and that you can concisely communicate it to anyone within the organization. For example, if your initial assignment is to provide specific expertise on a given engineering project, focus on and talk about that. Keep your eyes and ears open! But stay focused on what you were hired to do.

Help them look good. Most of your client's personnel want to do their share and be occasionally recognized. As an informed, objective outsider you may be able to legitimately compliment individuals directly and speak positively about them to others. But do not damage your credibility by offering unfounded compliments.

MEET PROMISED DELIVERABLES, SCHEDULE AND BUDGET

Add value to the assigned project. "Earn your keep." The challenge in managing any project—in this case, your first assignment with a new client—is simultaneously achieving three often "at odds" goals: deliverables, schedule and budget. Basic ideas on project management are presented in Chapter 9, the next chapter. If you have to "give" on any of the three goals, let it be budget, that is, your fee and/or expenses. In effect, accept a lower hourly rate than you had anticipated so that you deliver on deliverables and meet the schedule. This first assignment may, in effect, be your unplanned loss leader! Note: This advice assumes that you are not being asked to do much more than originally agreed upon.

LEVERAGE THIS FIRST ASSIGNMENT TO OBTAIN ADDITIONAL ASSIGNMENTS WITH THIS AND OTHER CLIENTS

This is the marketing aspect of any project that you do. Refer back to Chapter 7, "Marketing: Sleazy Activity or Mutually Beneficial Process?" Review those concepts, ideas, and tactics. Most of them are directly applicable to you and your new client. Have you or are you using them? Whose trust have you earned? What needs have you learned? How can you be of further service? Your second assignment with this new client probably lies within the answers to these questions.

Whether or not you receive one or more additional assignments from your new client, think of ways you can leverage this project to obtain similar projects with other clients. Some suggestions follow:

- Ask your principal client contact if you can use him or her as a reference when you present your credentials to other potential clients. Most clients will be pleased to provide this assistance.

- If the project or, more likely, parts of the project are unique, suggest that you and your principal contact write or present a paper. Look for an audience that is likely to include potential clients. Stress benefits in the paper and be prepared to do most of the work yourself. Recognize that papers and presentations co-authored with clients tend to have great credibility.

- If the paper is in written form, or is published, send copies to potential clients.

- Assuming you have a lead with another client, ask your current client, as a favor to you, to call his or her counterpart and discuss the project and your performance.

- If your project resulted in a constructed structure or facility, visit it with prospective clients. Arrange to have an owner's representative meet you at the site. If your project resulted in a manufactured product, show it to prospective clients and refer the client to product users. The proof is in the pudding. What could be more convincing to a potential client than a constructed project or manufactured product being endorsed by a proud owner?

- Assuming the project is noteworthy, suggest to your principal client contact that you jointly submit the project to a design or other competition. These competitions are typically arranged at the state or national levels by professional societies such as ASCE and the American Consulting Engineers Council (ACEC).

- Hire professionals to photograph and frame images of your project for display in your office. Even if few clients or potential clients see them, your ready access to the photographs will be a vivid reminder of what you have already accomplished as a free lancer.

The preceding suggestions are all actions that you can initiate. And you absolutely must do such things. Paralleling, and independent of your proactive marketing efforts, you may receive leads or assignments with other clients as a result of your first project with a client. For example, if your client is pleased with your service, he or she will tell others. Good news travels fast. Bad news travels even faster. Be thankful for, but do not count on chance and serendipity. They should supplement the proactive marketing efforts you undertake to leverage your projects. You must be in the driver's seat.

ALL GOOD THINGS COME TO AN END

Having stressed the importance of performing well again and again and again for each valued client, recognize that even very good things often come to an end. You and your long-term client may part ways for a variety of reasons, some uplifting and some discouraging.

Uplifting Separations

Consider first some possible positive reasons that you and your client go separate ways. Perhaps you provide management and leadership services to engineering and other technically oriented organizations. The CEO of one of your clients, who turned out to be a valued, long-term client, originally brought you on board to deal with some serious problems including lack of any heir apparent and conflict within senior management. Over a period of a year or so, you helped solve these problems and, as a result, worked yourself out of a job. So pin on a gold star and move on, probably with excellent references.

Or maybe you were retained to help start, either in an expert role or as a facilitator, a completely new program. Examples are designing and implementing a marketing plan for a new service or new geographic area or designing and implementing a new education and training program. With your help, the client designed and began implementation of the plan or program. You observe that the new endeavor is up and running, so you bow out because you are now adding very little value. Another gold star. As suggested by the preceding examples, sometimes the ultimate test of the quality of the job you do as a sole proprietor consultant is to "lose your job."

Discouraging Separations

Now consider some negative reasons why you and what was a long-term, valued client may go your separate ways. Recall the expression, "familiarity breeds contempt." This sort of thing can happen in the client-individual practitioner relationship. They simply get tired of having you around—after all, on any given bad day, you can be viewed as only an expense. Furthermore, whatever level of obligation they feel toward their own employees (and that level could be very low), they feel, and rightly so, even less obligation toward you. So thankfully move on, hopefully richer in both a monetary sense and an experience sense.

Another "grounds" for "divorce" is bad chemistry. You haven't changed all that much during the multi-year relationship, but the client has brought in a new, upper management person. You and he or she are incompatible. Again, you may decide to move on or your nemesis may directly or indirectly cause you to do so. Do so cheerfully being thankful that you don't have to work with that person.

A variation on the preceding, in that it involves one person on the client's staff, is when your key contact at the client moves on to other employment opportunities. If you haven't developed back-up relationships with one or more other influential personnel, your connection to the client may be broken. If this happens to you, view it as a well learned marketing lesson and vow to always cultivate more than one trusting connection with each client.

Another negative reason for separating could be what you view as matter of principle. This case is highly dependent on your standards and your level of tolerance. For example, your client may obtain scope or related ideas and information from you without compensating you and then use those deliverables to solicit qualifications or proposals from other consultants. You may find this unacceptable and decide to walk away from the client.

If you and a client part for what are referred to here as discouraging or negative reasons, you may be tempted to have great regrets and perhaps feel or even act bitter. This temptation is greater if other setbacks are simultaneously coming your way. Resist these impulses. Succumbing to them could adversely affect your other work and strain relationships with other clients and your business partners. Instead, be appreciative for what you learned and what you earned as a result of serving the now ex-client. Assuming you've maintained a smart, continuous marketing effort, as described in Chapter 7, new clients are waiting in the wings.

REVIEW

In summary, review the main points in this chapter "Tips on Being Successful With a New Client." Your first assignment with a client offers the very real possibility of a multi-year, mutually-beneficial relationship. Whether or not this happens will be determined primarily by you. Be prepared for suspicion and animosity. Counter such tendencies by focusing on your assignment and "earning your keep." Meet promised deliverables, schedule and budget. Creatively and proactively leverage your first assignment with a new client to secure additional projects with that client and with other clients. Remember that all good things come to an end including some long-term relationships with valued clients. Accordingly, market continuously.

A closing thought, offered by Pirsig (1974, p. 247) in his book *Zen and the Art of Motorcycle Maintenance*:

> *...care and quality are internal and external aspects of the same thing. A person who sees quality, and feels it as he works is a person who cares. A person who cares about what he sees and does is a person who's bound to have some characteristics of quality.*

If you truly care about your first project with a client and provide quality service, you will have successfully launched your sole proprietorship.

Chapter 9

Project Management

Why do we never have enough time to do it right but always have enough time to do it over? (Anonymous)

THIS IS NOT NEW TO YOU

If you are seriously thinking of starting a sole proprietorship, ***you already know much about project management.*** You've probably managed–or maybe mismanaged–your share of projects while employed by others. From experience, you understand the importance of project management, especially in the private sector. You know how project management impacts many aspects of the consulting business. Effective project management creates profit, produces a happy and satisfied client, reduces liability exposure, provides learning opportunities, leads to additional contracts with existing and new clients, and provides personal satisfaction (Walesh, 1996). Poor project management tends to cause the opposite.

Now, as an individual practitioner, project management will be even more important. Your livelihood will depend on how well you function as a project manager. You could, and maybe did, continue gainful employment within a government entity or consulting engineering firm without being an effective project manager. Those days are over! Now poor project management will at minimum, drive down your per hour, pre-tax income and, at maximum, drive away clients. Accordingly, a review of project management fundamentals is appropriate.

QUALITY DEFINED

> *Quality is free. It's not a gift, but it is free. What costs money are the unquality things—all the actions that involve not doing jobs right the first time.* (Crosby, 1979, p. 1)

Of course, clients want to receive "quality" and, of course, you, as a sole proprietor, want to deliver "quality." But what is quality? Consider three possible concepts.

Quality as Opulence

The word quality in the context of professional work or in a general context, may suggest opulence, luxury, "gold-plating," and over-design. Examples of products or results consistent with this opulence concept of quality might be Mercedes Benz automobiles, Rolex watches, cashmere sweaters, and safety factors of 3.0. That is, such products and results generally go well beyond what is needed for functional purposes, but not necessarily beyond what may be desired by a few individuals or organizations.

In an individual or organizational environment of unlimited, or at least great resources, the opulence definition or understanding of quality might be acceptable. The opulent approach to quality, however, is not useful in the vast majority of engineering and business situations that you will encounter as a free lancer.

Quality as Excellence or Superiority

Another approach to quality is the concept of excellence or superiority as suggested by the dictionary (Neufeldt, 1994) definition of quality which includes "...degree of excellence..." and "superiority." Offering a superior, standard-setting product or service is certainly admirable, but is not likely to be practical for most engineering and business situations. While clients may value "excellence" and "superiority," they may not want to pay for it. Furthermore, while notions of excellence and superiority may engender positive reactions, they may be both too vague and too expensive.

Nevertheless, some technical professionals will argue for a superiority approach to quality. As an example of this perspective, Huntington (1989), says "Quality, however, will not come from automation, but from obsession—a craftsman's obsession with making a thing as good as it can be made." While TQM advocates would agree that quality will not necessarily come from automation, they would tend to take great issue with the "as good as it can be made" understanding of quality.

Crosby (1979, p. 14), says, "The first erroneous assumption is that quality means goodness, or luxury, or shininess, or weight." Quality must mean something other than opulence or superiority in kind to the enlightened, progressive, but practical technical professional and/or businessperson. This leads to a third definition of quality and one that is widely accepted.

Quality as Meeting Requirements

Quality is conformance to requirements. Crosby (1979, p. 15) says, "We must define quality as conformance to requirements." Lewis (1998) elaborates by saying, "Quality is conformance to requirements. It is achieved by conforming to properly developed criteria which make the services meet all of the customer's needs and expectations." Snyder (1993, p. 53) offers this definition of quality:

> *Quality in engineering is a measure of how well engineering services meet the client's needs and conform to governing criteria and current practice standards.*

This definition is useful because it elaborates somewhat on the concept of "meeting requirements." Certainly, the client, owner or customer has a major role in defining requirements. But the definition of requirements may need to go beyond what the client, owner, or customer needs or believes they need. For example, the sole proprietor engineer must strive to satisfy government regulations, respect codes of ethics, and be consistent with the standard of care of the profession. In the final analysis, a potential client, owner, or customer's requirements may fall short of what the individual practitioner is willing or able to do. In such situations, personal and corporate ethical standards may require termination of the relationship.

Quality definitions used by professional organizations embody the same concepts. For example, the Quality Management Task Force of the Construction Industry Institute says, "Quality is conformance to established requirements." (Davis and Ledbetter, 1988). The "quality manual" of the American Society of Civil Engineers (ASCE, 1990, pp. 1-2), which focuses on achieving quality in the constructed project, states:

> *...quality is defined as meeting established requirements. Quality in the constructed project is achieved if the completed project conforms to the stated requirements of the principal participants (owner, design professional, constructor) while conforming to applicable codes, safety requirements, and regulations.*

Consider some hypothetical examples of quality as meeting requirements. If a Toyota Corolla meets a person's defined transportation needs, then, for that person, a Corolla is a better quality car than a Mercedes Benz. On the other hand, if a person's defined automobile transportation needs include leather upholstery, headlight wipers, and other special features typically found on the Mercedes Benz or other similar luxury automobiles, then the Corolla will clearly not meet the defined needs and will not be a quality product.

If a hand calculation of peak discharge from an industrial development using the rational method meets the design needs for sizing a length of storm sewer, then, for the client, the rational method is a better quality technique than a sophisticated hydrologic-hydraulic computer model. Or, to use a construction-related example quoted from the aforementioned ASCE Quality Manual (ASCE, 1990, p. 2):

> *Thus, a temporary, sheet-metal enhoused, pump station, with low capital cost, high operating costs, short expected life, and aesthetic deficiencies, may well be a quality project if it meets the expectations and requirements of the three principal participants. Conversely, a Taj Mahal with all of its beauty and durable materials may not qualify as a quality project if its construction results in costs or overruns, litigation, environmental controversy, or negative impact on public health and safety.*

Quality as meeting requirements, as opposed to quality as opulence or superiority, is widely used in business. You, as a sole proprietor, are advised to use this definition. It is the definition used in this book.

Frankly, technical professionals may have difficulty accepting the idea of quality as meeting, but not significantly exceeding, the established requirements. Almost any technical activity or project, such as field investigations, laboratory tests, a planning study, and a design culminating in plans and specifications for a manufactured product or constructed facility, can be done better than expected. After all, technical professionals tend to be very bright and usually have access to many and varied sophisticated tools and techniques. Furthermore, the technical professional's education may have encouraged him or her to go well beyond what was needed. But, in the world of practice and business, going well beyond what is needed tends to increase labor and other costs and cause delays, both of which are ultimately disruptive to a profitable business and to a satisfied customer or client. You need to weigh your personal desire to produce a superior or even opulent product or service against the best interests of your sole proprietorship business and those individuals or organizations that you serve.

Special situations are likely to arise in your sole proprietor business when you will go beyond client and other project requirements. There can be legitimate reasons for doing this. But be certain that you do it consciously with one or more specific business objectives in mind. At the other end of the "quality" spectrum, do not perform and deliver at a level that falls below quality as defined here.

EVERY PROJECT IS DONE TWICE

The common thread in project management should be, as stated by Covey (1990, p. 99), "the principle that all things are created twice. There is a mental or first creation, and a physical or second creation." Psychiatrist Sigmund Freud referred to the two-creation idea this way: "Thought is behavior in rehearsal." The remainder of this chapter emphasizes the value of the first creation with the conviction that, by so doing, there is a greatly enhanced probability that the second and ultimate creation will be achieved on time and within budget and will meet client and other project requirements.

PLAN YOUR WORK, WORK YOUR PLAN

Too many projects are done twice in a wasteful fashion. The first time through they, or major portions of them, are done wrong because of poor or no planning. Then they must be done a second time to get them right.

The premise of this chapter is that such waste and the associated frustration; loss of clients and customers, or constituents; and, for a sole proprietorship business, low or no profitability can be avoided by the philosophy "plan your work, work your plan." This productive way of doing a project twice is illustrated in FIGURE 9-1.

Although Pirsig (1974, p. 284), in his book *Zen and the Art of Motorcycle Maintenance*, describes a process ostensibly to use in a motorcycle repair project, his advice is applicable to project as used in this chapter. Before beginning the project, he in effect urges you, the sole proprietor, to:

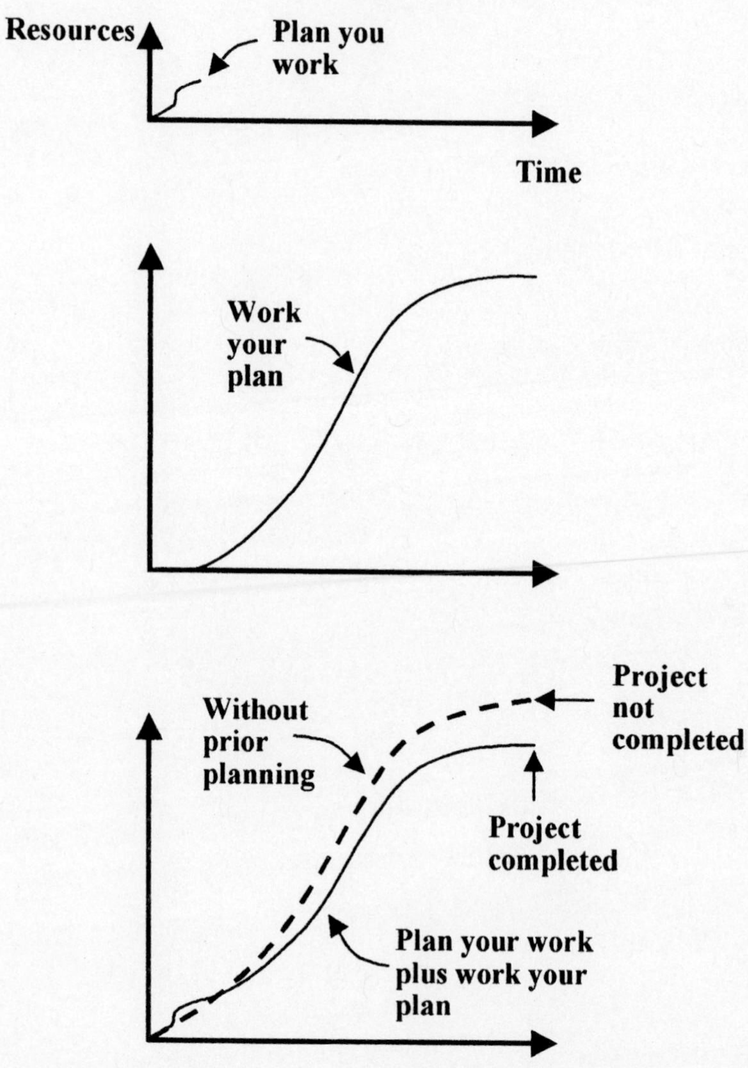

Figure 9-1. Plan your work and work your plan.

> *...list everything you're going to do on little slips of paper which you then organize into proper sequence. You discover that you organize and then reorganize the sequence again and again as more and more ideas come to you. The time spent that way usually more than pays for itself in time saved on the machine and prevents you from doing fidgety things that create problems later on.*

APPENDIX 9-1 is an example of a simple in-progress project plan. It is the project plan used by a sole proprietor for the project of planning, preparing for, conducting, and following up on a seminar. Note that each task begins with a verb. This helps to focus the user on useful, productive actions.

While you can go well beyond this simple model, do at least this much for all of your projects. Plan your work and then work your plan. A final thought on project plans. File project plans for completed projects. Retrieve selected ones as you plan new projects, thereby leveraging what you learned on earlier projects.

REVIEW

In closing this chapter titled "Project Management," reflect on the key ideas. Poor project management by you, as a free lancer, will at minimum, drive down your per hour income and, at maximum, drive away clients. Great project management is based on a clear understanding of and focus on quality. Quality means knowing and meeting requirements. Project requirements are not totally defined by the client. Every project is done twice. The smart way to do a project twice is to plan your work (the first or mental creation) and then work your plan (the second or physical creation). The not so smart way to do your project twice is to do it, or a major portion of it, poorly and then have to do it again to get it right.

Consider this anonymous thought:

> *P^6: Prior proper planning prevents poor performance.*

Appendix 9-1. Simple Project Plan

The following project plan was used by a sole proprietor for planning, preparing for, conducting and following up on a seminar.

PROJECT PLAN
FOR
JANUARY 1999 ASCE "MAKING $" SEMINAR
(Last update: 1/16/99)

- Set topics and dates with ASCE (DONE)
- Develop work plan (DONE)
- Set up files (DONE)
- Outline seminar and identify existing and possible sources of material (DONE)
- Prepare text for ASCE marketing materials (DONE)
- Arrange subcontractor for text and graphics preparation (DONE)
- Confirm that seminar is "a go" (DONE, Yes, as of 12/31/98)
- Arrange transportation (DONE)
- Arrange lodging (DONE)
- Draft and final "Making $" notebook
    - Cover (DONE)
    - Contents/schedule (DONE)

  - o Unit 1 (DONE)
  - o Unit 2 (DONE)
  - o Unit 3 (DONE)
  - o Unit 4 (STARTED)
  - o Unit 5 (DONE)
  - o Unit 6 (DONE)
  - o Unit 7 (STARTED)
  - o Unit 8 (DONE)
  - o Unit 9 (DONE)
  - o Unit 10 (DONE)

- Send new/revised text/graphics to subconsultant (DONE)
- Obtain final estimate of number of participants by Friday, 1/15/99 (NOT DONE)
- Acquire dividers
- Complete camera ready materials by Monday 1/18/99
- Arrange, through ASCE, for binders, cover and spine inserts (DONE)
- Copy and assemble materials minus loose-leaf notebooks
- Arrange AV and related logistics (DONE)
- Obtain information on ASCE's on-site representative
- Prepare for presentation
- Check out AV and other facilities
- Conduct seminar on Friday, 1/21/99
- Conduct evaluation (ASCE)
- Review evaluations provided by ASCE

- Note seminar revisions partly in response to evaluations
- Send invoice
- Follow-up with ASCE as needed
- Follow-up with participants as requested/promised

Chapter 10

Business and Personal Accounting: Keeping Financial Score

Profit is like health. You need it, and the more the better. But it is not why you exist. (Peters and Waterman, 1982, p. 103)

BACKGROUND

Accounting is the process of recording, summarizing, analyzing, verifying, and reporting in monetary terms the transactions of a business or other organization. Kamm (1989, p. 84) states that accountants are like journalists—they report what happens. In contrast with engineers and other technical professionals, who tend to make things happen, accountants normally record what has happened, at least the financial aspects.

Engineers and other technical professionals tend to be prospective and accountants retrospective.

The purpose of this chapter is to provide the potential sole proprietor with an introduction to basic accounting terminology and concepts. Two important financial statements—the balance sheet and the income statement—are discussed, as is the relationship between them. Time utilization rates, expense ratio, and the multiplier, accounting-related performance indicators for consulting engineering firms and similar service organizations, are discussed with emphasis on implications for the prospective sole proprietor. The income statement is discussed further, this time as part of the business plan for a professional services firm, including a sole proprietorship. The chapter concludes with advice on invoicing, getting paid and recording income and expenses.

BALANCE SHEET: HOW MUCH ARE YOU WORTH?

The balance sheet is one of several financial statements that define the financial condition of entities ranging from corporations to individuals. A personal balance sheet is a way for a sole proprietor to keep overall financial score, to determine if his or her net worth is growing rapidly enough.

A balance sheet is prepared at regular intervals such as monthly, quarterly, and annually; and can meet internal and external needs. Unfortunately, the balance sheet is referred to by other names (e.g., Clough, 1986, p. 263) such as financial statement, statement of financial condition, statement of worth, and statement of assets and liabilities. The term balance sheet is used in this chapter because the term seems appropriately descriptive and because it is widely used in engineering literature (e.g., Clough, 1986, p. 265; Kamm, 1989, p. 84).

The balance sheet shows, for a point in time, assets (A), liabilities (L), and net worth (NW) or equity (E). The basic equation for the balance sheet is:

$$A - L = NW \text{ (or E)}$$

An example balance sheet is presented and discussed in order to illustrate the features and usefulness of balance sheets. It is a hypothetical balance sheet for personal finances. Refer to FIGURE 10-1. This accounting of assets and liabilities could apply to a young professional and possibly his or her spouse within a year or so after graduation from college. Two observations are in order.

- First, balance sheets in general are not as accurate as they may appear to be, particularly when line items are entered to the nearest cent. For consistency purposes, accountants usually show all items to the nearest cent. Some line items such as the current balance of a checking account or the amount owed on an automobile loan, can be determined and stated to the nearest cent. However, in general, the overall accuracy of a balance sheet is less than that because some values are estimates such as the current market value of a condominium or other personal property. The accuracy inconsistency in a balance sheet is further complicated by the difficulty of getting all values to be simultaneous or coincident. However, accuracy variation does not detract from the usefulness of the balance sheet.

Assets		
Condominium	$110,000.00	
Personal property (e.g., furniture)	15,000.00	
XYZ stock	5,283.68	
Car	10,000.00	
Retirement (vested)	17,500.21	
Cash/checking	893.76	
Insurance (cash value)	1,012.16	
Total:	$159,689.81	(A)

Liabilities		
Mortgage on condo (SPW[1] of remaining payments)	$55,293.32	
Car loan (SPW)	7,151.98	
Credit cards	2,542.99	
College loan (SPW)	2,016.14	
Total:	$67,004.43	(L)

Net worth (or equity):	$92,685.38	(NW)

1) Series present worth

Figure 10-1. An end-of-calendar-year personal balance sheet provides an estimate of net worth.

- Second, while absolute values of line items, assets, and liabilities at any time are important, changes and trends such as a gradual increase in net worth for an individual, a couple, or a company are even more important. A balance sheet is a snapshot of net worth at a point in time. A series of balance sheets provides a moving picture of a changing and hopefully improving situation. For example, a young professional might exhibit a negative net worth shortly after graduation from college, but as a result of sound personal financial management, quickly improves the situation so that in a few years assets exceed liabilities and the difference grows.

If you have not already done so, you should develop a balance sheet for your personal finances. Consider using spreadsheet software to construct your balance sheet. Update your balance sheet, on an annual basis, by adding a column for the end of the current year. By preparing a balance sheet now and periodically updating it you will have a measure of how well you are managing your personal finances. You will also have ready access to the kinds of asset and liability data typically required by banks and other lending institutions in support of applications for home mortgages, automobile loans, business loans, and other common financial transactions. The personal balance sheet will also be an indication of how well you are managing income from your individual proprietorship. That's your real "bottom line."

INCOME STATEMENT: INCOME MINUS EXPENSES

The income statement is another important type of financial statement used in business. Recall that the balance sheet had other names. Unfortunately, so does the income statement which, as noted by Clough (1986, p. 261) is sometimes referred to as the profit and loss statement, statement of earnings, statement of loss and gain, income sheet, summary of income and expense, profit and loss summary, statement of operations, and operating statement. The term income statement is used in this chapter for simplicity and because it appears to be in common usage.

The income statement shows the type and amount of income and expense, along with the difference, over a specified period of time. Any time period is possible, but typically income statements are prepared on a monthly, quarterly, or annual basis. The basic equation for the income statement is:

Income - Expenses = Net Income

Two example income statements are presented. The first one applies to an individual's personal income and the second applies to a consulting business.

Refer to FIGURE 10-2, which might apply to a professional and his or her spouse. This income statement might be for the hypothetical young couple whose balance sheet is presented in FIGURE 10-1. However, there are no obvious connections between the two financial statements. Note, again, that the income statement shows income received and expenses incurred over a period of time. Contrast this with the balance sheet, which shows assets and liabilities at a point in time.

A personal income statement like that shown in FIGURE 10-2, could be used in a post-mortem mode to review income and expenses during the past year. In addition, a personal income statement could also be used in a prospective mode to plan income and its use in the near future. Retrospective and prospective uses of income statements are routinely made in the business environment.

Income			
Salaries (gross)		$60,052.29	
Interest/dividends		483.68	
Sale of stock		1,108.23	
	Total:	$61,644.20	(I)

Expenses			
Mortgage (interest and principal)		$9,406.16	
Utilities		2,829.00	
Food		3,500.00	
Clothing		2,500.00	
Car Payments		3,611.89	
Insurance		3,421.08	
Taxes		16,500.00	
Entertainment/travel		3,500.00	
	Total:	$45,268.13	(E)

	Net income	$16,376.07	(NI)

Figure 10-2. This hypothetical personal annual income statement shows income, expenses and net income for a year.

The observation made earlier about the variation in accuracy of line items in the balance sheet also applies to the income statement. For example, while items such as salaries and interest and dividends earned can be listed to the nearest penny, expense items such as entertainment/travel and clothing would be estimates unless unusually meticulous records are kept. Variation of accuracy within the income statement does not in any significant way detract from its usefulness as an analysis and planning tool.

INCOME STATEMENT AS PART OF THE BUSINESS PLAN FOR A SOLE PROPRIETORSHIP: DETERMINING YOUR HOURLY BILLING RATE

An income statement should be part of the first year's business plan for your contemplated sole proprietorship. Other typical elements of your business plan are market analysis, description of services to be offered, assessment of competition, and means of finance (e.g., see also Fenske and Fenske, 1989). These topics are introduced in Chapters 3 and 5.

You can now use accounting basics to create various income statement scenarios for the first year of your potential sole proprietorship. One result of each scenario will be an indication of your charge-out rates, that is, how much you will bill for each hour of your services. This is a ***prospective*** use of the income statement.

At the end of the year, you should prepare a ***retrospective*** (actual) income statement. You will need this for preparing your income taxes. More importantly, this retrospective income statement will quantify your actual fiscal performance. More specifically, what was your per hour before tax income? Was the first year worth the effort? Do you want to continue?

Example Prospective Income Statement

But, we are getting ahead of ourselves. One scenario of a hypothetical prospective, annual income statement for a sole proprietor follows:

1. Desired annual raw (before tax, no benefits included) "salary:" $70,000. This might be approximately equal to your current salary as an employee.

2. Portion of year to be devoted to the sole proprietorship (i.e., full time or part-time): 100%

3. Raw labor rate ($70,000)/(52 weeks x 40 hrs/week): $33.65/hour. Divide your desired annual salary as a sole proprietor by the total number of hours you plan to devote to your business.

4. Expected time utilization rate: 50%. Time utilization rate, also referred to as chargeable rate or billable rate, is the percent of hours you will work that will be billed directly to clients. A low rate (50%) is selected because this is the first year of your new business. You should eventually be able to achieve a time utilization rate of 75% or more.

5. Billable labor cost (0.50 x $70,000): $35,000. You want to earn $70,000 for your labor, but only half of it will be directly billable to clients. You will have to mark it up, but by how much?

6. Annual non-billable labor cost ($70,000 – $35,000): $35,000

7. Annual non-billable, non-labor costs:

- Office space rental (125 ft^2 x \$12/ft^2): \$ 1,500
- Travel: 3,000
- Computer hardware, software, supplies, training: 5,000
- Other office equipment: 1,000
- Marketing materials: 1,000
- Benefits (e.g., retirement, medical insurance): 10,000
- Miscellaneous: 1,500
- Total: \$23,000

The preceding costs will not be explicitly reimbursed by clients during projects.

8. Total overhead (No. 6 + No. 7, that is, \$35,000 + \$23,000): \$58,000

9. Overhead ratio (overhead/billable direct labor or No. 8/No. 6 or \$58,000/\$35,000): 1.66

10. Necessary total revenue:

Billable labor cost:	\$35,000
Overhead:	58,000
Total revenue:	\$93,000

11. Necessary multiplier (Total revenue/billable direct labor = M = 93,000/35,000): 2.66. The multiplier is used to mark up the raw labor rate.

12. Charge out rate (multiplier x raw labor rate = 2.66 x $33.65/hr): $89.42/hr.

Is scenario 1 realistic? In answering this look closely at the reasonableness of the desired annual raw "salary" ($70,000), the likelihood of achieving the time utilization rate (50%), the acceptability of the necessary charge out rate ($89.42/hr.), and various suspect assumptions. If scenario 1 is not realistic, what change might be considered for scenario 2?

A Simpler Version of the Income Statement

The preceding prospective income statement generating process may seem unnecessarily complex. A simpler, six-step approach to a sole proprietor's prospective income statement is as follows: It applies to the first year of business.

1. Desired annual raw "salary," that is, before taxes with no benefits included: $70,000

2. Total number of hours (billable and non-billable, including vacation) you expect to work in a year (52 weeks x 40 hrs/week): 2080 hours

3. Expected number of total hours that will be billable (50% or 0.50 x 2080 hours): 1040 hours

4. Expenses, non-reimbursables (See Item 7 in preceding analysis): $23,000

5. Total necessary income before taxes (salary + non-reimbursable expenses or $70,000 + $23,000): $93,000

6. Charge out rate (total necessary income divided by billable hours or $93,000 / 1040hrs): $89.42/hr.

So How Much Do Others Charge?

A 1999 survey of architectural, engineering, environmental and planning firms by Zweig White and Associates provides some general hourly rate data (NSPE, 1999). Based on polling of "…hundreds of top managers," the following median hourly billing rates were reported:

Category	Median Hourly Rate ($)	
	1998	1999
Engineers	60	65
Architects	60	65
Project Managers	85	88
Associates	90	97
Department Heads	90	100
Principals	115	120

Based on your area of expertise and range of experience, the preceding hourly rates can serve as a check on the reasonableness of the rates you plan to use. For additional details on the 1999 survey, refer to the original report (Zweig White, 1999).

Case Study

Bergeron (1999) presents a hypothetical case study of a disastrous sole proprietorship startup. Because it focuses on the income statement for the sole proprietor, it is an informative extension of material presented in this chapter. Useful lessons illustrated by the case study are:

- Don't borrow too much money too quick.
- Update a projected income statement to reflect reality.

- Track cash flow.
- Establish a high enough billing rate.
- Market continuously and intelligently.
- Invoice frequently.
- Get paid.

DON'T "GIVE YOUR TIME AWAY"

You, as an honest, conscientious sole proprietor who generates income primarily by billing time, will have difficulty billing an average of eight hours per work day. Even six will be a challenge. Oh, there will be 60 hours billed some weeks when the "crunch" is on. However, over the long haul, billing 40, or even 30 hours, per week will be a challenge.

This is not to say that you won't be working 40, 50, or even 60 hours per week. However, many essential, but non-billable tasks will require your attention and time. Examples are marketing, continuing education, administration (e.g., "doing your taxes" or working with someone who is providing the service), professional activities that are not primarily marketing but are important to you, and vacation.

When working on a full-time job for a salary, the assumption is that you are earning on the basis of producing 40 hours per week. When working as an individual practitioner and conscientiously billing time actually worked to various clients, accumulating even six hours per day of billable time is challenging.

One bit of advice, so that you don't permit your clients to unintentionally "nickel and dime" you. Have this billing policy: whenever you have to quickly "switch gears" to another project (e.g., in response to a telephone call from a client), bill a minimum of 0.25 hours. The generous side of you may be tempted to say, "Oh, the call only took five or ten minutes so I'll forget about it." In that five or ten minutes you probably did two things: provided timely and useful ideas, information or guidance to or for your client and were abruptly pulled away from the other project. You now have to "come back up to speed" on the other project. Consider including a statement like the following in your agreements or on invoices: "Minimum of 0.25 hours per task."

Failing to follow the preceding advice, or something similar, will result in days in which you worked hard delivering value to many clients in various ways but have little to show for it in billable hours.

ALTERNATIVES TO SELLING TIME

Buying Labor Wholesale and Selling it Retail: The Limitation of Being Paid by the Hour

The dominant revenue and, hopefully, profit-making mode for many consulting firms is to invoice by the hour plus expenses. These firms buy labor wholesale (the raw labor rates of their employees) and mark it up with a multiplier to sell it (bill it) retail. With this arrangement, no matter how effective a firm's time utilization, its potential profit is limited by the buy wholesale – sell retail process. Consulting firm profits are not necessarily limited by the value of the services delivered but rather by tying the services to the hours required to deliver them. In a sense, most consulting firms are selling time, not services.

Being Open to Other Ways of Packaging and Pricing Services

You, as a sole proprietor, can follow the same "selling time" mode that dominates the consulting business. The "selling time" approach is inherent in the preceding sections of this chapter beginning with the discussion of the income statement as part of the business plan for a sole proprietorship.

However, there are alternatives to selling time for consulting firms and for you, as an individual practitioner. Now, at the beginning of your free lance business, is the appropriate time to study possible other ways to package and price services for enhanced profit. You should seek ways to leverage your knowledge and experience so that you get compensated for its value to clients, not for the hours required to deliver it.

The options presented here are not unique to the sole proprietor consultant. They could, and some are, being employed by consulting firms. However, you have the ultimate in autonomy to experiment. Outlined here are the following four alternatives:

- Lump sum contract
- Retainer agreement
- Pay for performance
- Knowledge products

Lump Sum Contract

As explained by Lindeburg (1997, p. 57), "The lump sum or fixed fee structure is most suitable for relatively small engagements in which the required services are clearly specified." Explicit in this definition is the fact that profitable lump sum contracting depends, in part, on your and the client's ability to define and agree upon the scope and deliverables. By doing so, you have recourse if the client asks for extras.

Not obvious, but implicit, in the preceding definition of lump sum contracting is that it can be very profitable. Two profitable possibilities come to mind.

- Efficient process: Consider the lump sum approach in situations where you have developed and fine-tuned a process for delivering a particular service. Because of technology and your experience and discipline, you can meet client requirements with less resources (time and expense) than the competition. You price the service approximately as they would but do it for less cost and reap a larger profit. Of course, if you really "need the work," you may be tempted to price it for less than the competition to improve the probability of winning the assignment. You still make a profit, albeit a smaller one.

- Unique service: Consider the lump sum approach when you offer a unique or rare service. There is little or no equal competition. You price the service at a level corresponding to the client's value of it, assuming that is well above the costs you would incur in delivering the service.

Assume you are fortunate to secure a lump sum contract for an amount that is well above, maybe even multiples of your delivery cost. This is true value pricing in that the client values the services at the agreed upon lump sum amount. You are being rewarded for fine tuning your process for delivering services or for your foresight in recognizing needs and creating a unique or rare service to meet those needs. Enjoy the fruits of your labor while recognizing that other, less imaginative consultants will soon follow.

A financially significant advantage of lump sum agreements over hourly plus expenses with not-to-exceed agreements is that the former provide for recovery of some marketing hours and marketing expenses. Assume you've devoted X hours and spent Y dollars following up on a lead. You have earned an invitation to submit a priced proposal, hopefully on a sole source basis.

If you are pricing your services on a lump sum basis, you can include some or all of the hours invested and the dollars spent to date in developing the project. Doing so may also result in a proposed lump sum fee that is unacceptably high to the client. Presumably you have the business sense needed to assess the situation.

In contrast, if you are preparing an hourly plus expenses with a not-to-exceed proposal, you typically cannot plan to bill hours and expenses that were incurred prior to the signing of an agreement, unless explicitly agreed to by the client. Why? Because such agreements typically require that invoices include an accounting of hours worked and expenses incurred subsequent to formalizing the agreement.

Lump sum pricing facilitates legally and ethically recouping all or some pre-agreement marketing labor and expenses. An hourly plus expenses with a not-to-exceed typically precludes compensation for pre-agreement labor and expenses.

In summary, positive aspects of lump sum contracting for the free lancer include:

- Potential for much more than the standard profit.

- Opportunity to recoup some marketing labor and expenses.

- Simpler billing process, although not necessarily a simpler time and expense record keeping process.

The principal negative feature of lump sum arrangements for the sole proprietor is the need to work with the potential client to clearly define and agree upon scope and deliverables. However, clear understanding of scope and deliverables is also essential for the more common hourly plus expenses with a not-to-exceed amount.

Finally, clients often prefer lump sum contracts for two reasons. First, they have, up front, a better idea of the total cost of services. Second, there is less need to carefully review invoices.

Retainer Agreement

Lindeburg (1997, p. 56) writes "A retainer may be appropriate when a client needs consulting engineering services on a continuing or recurring basis. You may agree to provide these services on call in exchange for a set fee."

A retainer agreement recognizes and compensates you for your expertise and your on-call availability. It might be exclusive, that is, you agree to provide a particular service or set of services to only one client for a specified time period. Included in the retainer agreement should be a provision for additional compensation or expense reimbursement if agreed upon limits are exceeded. Retainer payments could be made on a monthly or annual basis.

One example of a retainer situation would be troubleshooting a problematic wastewater treatment plant. In this case, the client might be a municipality. Another retainer example arrangement would be assisting a consulting firm in preparing proposals for large projects within a specific technical discipline or service line. In this case, the retainer agreement might be exclusive because your availability gives the consulting firm a competitive advantage.

The retainer arrangement is likely to be more profitable then the "selling hours" approach. It should be because you are committing to being on call, however that is defined. Furthermore, the retainer agreement may be exclusive with the client. Retainer agreements will not be less profitable than "selling hours" because of the upset limits typically included.

Pay for Performance

With this service pricing and packaging option, you provide a service, the success of which can be measured monetarily. If successful, your contract prescribes compensation in proportion to the success. A hypothetical example is a mechanical engineer being retained by an industrial client to reduce energy costs at a manufacturing facility. He or she might contract to receive X% of the first year's savings and Y% of the second year's savings.

Another example is a management consultant contracts to assist an engineering consulting firm increase its profitability. In this case the consultant might be compensated on the basis of a percent of the improved profit over a year or so.

Knowledge Products

Examples of knowledge products include newsletters (traditional and electronic), audio/video cassettes, manuals/handbooks/books, workshops, and web-based training (WBT). To explore this possibility, carefully assess your knowledge, your experience and the materials you have produced that you own. Imagine ways that they could be packaged and marketed to meet current or imminent needs.

A negative aspect of offering knowledge products is that you will probably have to make a significant up-front investment of labor and expense to assemble, package, and market the product. Furthermore, there is no guarantee that there will be a return on the investment. Finally, you may be concerned about providing competitors access to what you view as unique or special data, information, and approaches.

There are several potential positive features of knowledge products. Most notable are the following:

- While you "sell" some of your knowledge, you still retain it. Furthermore, the "latest and greatest" is soon not the "latest and greatest." Knowledge is evolving, if not dynamic, within the realm of engineers and other technical professionals. Satisfied buyers may return again and again for updates.

- Because of the publicity associated with the marketing of knowledge products, your role as an expert will be enhanced. This exposure could strengthen the market for and value of your more traditional consulting services.

- You could do very well financially. If one of your products proves to be popular, the incremental costs of producing or manufacturing more copies will tend to be very small which means that the profit per unit will be very high.

A final thought about knowledge products. Creating and marketing them is increasingly within the grasp of free lancers because of ever-expanding computer hardware and software and electronic communication. For example, you, as a sole proprietor, working by yourself and probably using some carefully selected subcontracted services, can:

- Create, market, and conduct a workshop
- Offer an electronic newsletter
- Self-publish a book and market it over the Internet
- Create a website

INVOICING

Frequency

You may be tempted, on projects of one to several months duration, to simply send one invoice at the end of the project. While this practice may simplify your and your client's accounting efforts, it may create serious cash flow problems for you. The problem will be aggravated if this is your only project or your principal project. Income could cease for several months.

Invoicing monthly is a more prudent practice with less frequent invoicing being reserved for special situations. One example of such situations is when the invoice amount would be so small as to not warrant your effort to prepare the invoice and your client's effort to process it. Another possible exception to monthly invoicing is when nothing substantive has been delivered to a very sensitive client.

Invoice a new client as soon as possible, subject to the preceding considerations. If there are any misunderstandings between you and your client, the first invoice may reveal them. Regardless of how careful you've been in starting the relationship with a new client, loose ends may exist. Examples of areas of potential misunderstandings are the type of expenses that are passed on to the client for reimbursement, the number of hours billed for meetings, and the adequacy of invoice documentation.

Reporting Project Status

In a related matter, the invoice provides an opportunity to go beyond documenting labor and expenses. Depending on the project and the client, consider including a synopsis of the project status with the invoice. Do this only if it will serve a specific, value-added purpose.

Note key tasks completed, principal deliverables, problems encountered and how they have or will be resolved, and planned activities. Status reports may be appreciated by your client contact, especially if he or she has to, in turn, report internally on the status of contract projects.

GETTING PAID

Assuming you are prudent in the selection of clients (the selection process does go both ways), almost all invoices will be paid in a reasonable time. You can further reduce the likelihood of non-payment or problematic payment by taking certain actions when you prepare invoices. Even more importantly, you and your client should address certain invoicing logistics well before you submit your first invoice. Presented here are suggestions on early actions as well as ideas to consider at the time of invoicing. These tips are taken, in part, from Olden (1991) and Stone (1999).

Early Actions

Depending on the situation (e.g., first project for a client contrasted with another project with a long term client), consider discussing or doing the following well before you intend to submit the first invoice:

- Negotiate an initial payment, due at the time of signing or otherwise formalizing the agreement. The amount might be the larger of the expected monthly fee or 10% of the total estimated fee. The intent is to have the initial payment applied to the final invoice.

- Agree on frequency of invoicing. If invoicing is to be based on completion of project phases, rather than periodically, negotiate a sufficient number of phases.

- Learn the optimum time to submit invoices. For example, if the client normally "cuts checks" on the 21st day of the month, time your invoices so that they arrive just soon enough before that date to be reviewed and approved.

- Consider establishing a late payment interest charge. This is a sensitive issue not necessarily because of the money involved but more likely because of the implied mistrust of your client. Use discretion in even suggesting this.

- Establish systematic steps to be taken if payment is not received in a timely fashion. Withhold necessary signatures and/or sections of documents. Like the preceding possible action, this one is sensitive. Again, use discretion.

- Determine the format of the invoice, preferably by using an example. Agree on the level of detail and the amount of documentation to be provided.

- Perform proactively on the project and meet requirements. This creates goodwill and encourages the client to quickly approve payment of invoices.

Actions During Invoicing

The following ideas apply to the actual preparation of invoices:

- Issue invoices periodically and at about the same time to establish a pattern and momentum.

- If different parts (e.g., labor vs. reimbursable expenses) of the total invoice have to be approved by different client personnel, consider separate invoices, that is, one for labor and one for expenses.

- If invoices require approval of two or more client personnel, consider simultaneously sending the original to one person with clearly marked copies to the other individuals.

- If your invoices typically contain two or more subtotals and/or run two or more pages, make it easy for the reviewer to find the total amount due. For example, regardless of where else the total amount due appears, place it near the beginning of the invoice. Failure to follow this suggestion may result in someone inadvertently sending you a check for one of your subtotals. This, in turn, requires time-consuming corrective actions by you and your client.

- Present an invoice that meets all previously agreed upon requirements, is user-friendly, and has a professional appearance.

- Make a paper or electronic copy of the invoice, including documentation, so that you can readily respond to client questions.

RECORDING INCOME AND EXPENSES

As noted by Perlstein (1998, p. 43), when you become a sole proprietor "you are the accounting department." He goes on to say:

> *Start by talking with a CPA. Find out all the requirements you'll have to meet to be prepared at tax time. While IRS regulations are complex, bookkeeping for free lancers doesn't have to be.*

Categories

As the calendar year progresses, you will need to record three classes of accounting data:

1. ***Invoices paid***, noting in particular, the part that is your fee because this is potentially taxable income. You will also want to keep track of invoices not paid. Don't let them go too long! However, assuming you are operating on a cash basis, normal unpaid invoices are not relevant to income taxes.

2. ***Expenses you incur***. There are two types:

    - Expenses that ***are reimbursed*** by your clients. These depend on your arrangement with clients and might include items such as travel, lodging, telephone and fax, and high volume copying. While you should try to get as large a fraction of expenses as possible in the reimbursable category, that desire must be balanced against the effort required to monitor and document those expenses.

- Expenses that ***are not reimbursed*** by your clients. This is your overhead and will be deducted from your income to determine your taxable income. Examples of typically non-reimbursable expenses include office supplies, computer hardware and software, and office rental. Perlstein (1998, p. 44) wisely suggests organizing or aggregating your non-reimbursable expenses in the categories used on Schedule C of Internal Revenue Service (IRS) Form 1040. This will facilitate preparation of the sole proprietor portion of your federal income tax form. Schedule C is included as APPENDIX 10-1.

3. The ***total number of hours*** devoted to your business. Include billable hours for which you received payment. Also include non-billable hours in your record keeping. Examples include the time you devote to administration, marketing, and continuing education. You must know the total number of hours invested in your professional services business for the calendar year. This total will enable you to calculate your actual pre-tax hourly income. Pre-tax hourly income is the most meaningful measure of how well you are doing. For example, compare it to what you previously earned as an employee. Track pre-tax

hourly income on an annual basis as an indication of how well you are doing.

Another reason for faithfully recording income and expenses, especially in the first and other growing years of your sole proprietorship, is that you must make approximately quarterly estimated income tax payments during the calendar year to cover income taxes. These payments are made to federal, state and sometimes local entities. About one-fourth of your estimated total tax obligation for the current calendar year must be sent to the IRS and usually the state equivalent on April 15, June 15, September 15 and January 15. Note that the dates are not exactly quarterly. They can "sneak up on you."

A System

Develop a system to track and document business income and expenses. Options include commercial software, such as Quick Books or Money, or your own specially-designed spreadsheet (Zbar, 2000). Whatever system you employ, select/design and use it in anticipation of meeting end-of-the-year tax filing requirements.

To the extent feasible, log income and expenses into your system as they occur. You are less likely to make errors. Furthermore, you will have a more accurate picture of how you are doing.

Although the U.S. Tax Code doesn't require sole proprietors to open a separate checking account or carry a separate credit card, you may want to do so. In contrast, business entities like partnerships and corporations do need separate checking accounts (Zbar, 2000).

Real Time Accounting

Experience suggests that your accounting will be more accurate, require less time, provide a more accurate indication of your income, and be more acceptable to the IRS if your accounting actions are done contemporaneously or, at best, as soon as possible. A contemporaneous approach means that expenses and income are recorded and, as necessary, documented in real time. Some examples:

- You purchase office supplies. You obtain a receipt and immediately file it physically in a month-by-month file system. At the end of each month, you enter this and all other expenses into your custom made or other accounting system.

- You receive a check as payment on an invoice. You immediately deposit the check into your checking account and then, or at the end of the month, enter the income and reimbursable expenses into your accounting system.

As noted, one of the four advantages of this contemporaneous or as-soon-as-possible approach is that it is more accurate. You are less likely to forget an expense or lose documentation if your process it immediately.

The second advantage to the suggested approach is that you are likely to spend less total time on accounting and related documentation if you process it in real time or as soon as feasible. This is a more efficient use of your time than trying to remember and reconstruct events days and weeks later.

The third benefit of contemporaneous or soon-as-possible accounting is that it gives you a current picture of how well you are doing at any time of the year. By seeing your net, pre-tax income to date, you can project your net pre-tax income for the year. You will also have a basis for determining the size of quarterly tax payments.

The fourth and final benefit of the suggested approach is that it is likely to help you work with the IRS if you are audited. For example, small expenses not documented by receipts are more likely to be allowed by the IRS if you demonstrate that you routinely record expenses as they occur.

RETIREMENT

Using the balance sheet recommendations presented in this chapter, monitor (on at least an annual basis) and project your net worth. The bottom line question is: will your net worth be sufficient at retirement? Set up a retirement program. One option is a Simplified Employee Program (SEP) which allows you to invest, in an income shielded fashion, up to 13% of your income in a retirement program. You pay no taxes on the amount invested or on the earnings until you draw from your retirement fund. Contact a financial advisor for additional information.

REVIEW

In summary, review the main points in this chapter "Business and Personal Accounting: Keeping Financial Score." Success as a sole proprietor requires basic knowledge of personal and business accounting. Accounting is the mechanism for keeping your financial score. Your personal net worth, and possibly the net worth of your business, are quantified by means of balance sheets. You should develop a personal balance sheet and update it at least annually. It is essential to monitoring your overall financial situation and projecting your retirement options. The income statement is the basis for understanding time utilization, expense ratios, multipliers, and profitability in the consulting business. Used in a prospective mode, the projected income statement for your sole proprietorship helps establish hourly rates for your new free lance business. Don't "give your time away" and do explore alternatives to selling time. Invoice frequently and use sound business practices to make sure you get paid.

As part of your role as the "accounting department" for your free lance business, you will need to record, as the calendar year progresses, invoices paid, expenses that were reimbursed, non-reimbursed expenses, non-billable hours, and billable hours for which you received payment. This is, in effect, the income statement in the retrospective mode. You will also need to make approximately quarterly estimated income tax payments to the IRS, probably to the state, and maybe to local entities. Annual pre-tax hourly income is a simple index to how well you are doing. To the extent feasible, embrace real time accounting. Plan for and fund your retirement.

Consider this closing thought offered by W. Edwards Deming:

> *Profit in business comes from repeat customers, customers that boast about your project or service, and that bring friends with them.*

Appendix 10-1. IRS Schedule C

(1 of 4)

SCHEDULE C
(Form 1040)

Department of the Treasury
Internal Revenue Service (10)

Profit or Loss From Business

(Sole Proprietorship)

▶ **Partnerships, joint ventures, etc., must file Form 1065 or Form 1065-B.**

▶ **Attach to Form 1040 or Form 1041.** ▶ **See Instructions for Schedule C (Form 1040).**

OMB No. 1545-0074

1999

Attachment
Sequence No. **09**

Name of proprietor | **Social security number (SSN)**

A Principal business or profession, including product or service (see page C-1) | **B Enter code from pages C-8 & 9** ▶

C Business name. If no separate business name, leave blank. | **D Employer ID number (EIN), if any**

E Business address (including suite or room no.) ▶
City, town or post office, state, and ZIP code

F Accounting method: **(1)** ☐ Cash **(2)** ☐ Accrual **(3)** ☐ Other (specify) ▶

G Did you "materially participate" in the operation of this business during 1999? If "No," see page C-2 for limit on losses . ☐ **Yes** ☐ **No**

H If you started or acquired this business during 1999, check here . . . . . ▶ ☐

Part I Income

1	Gross receipts or sales. **Caution:** *If this income was reported to you on Form W-2 and the "Statutory employee" box on that form was checked, see page C-2 and check here* ▶ ☐	1	
2	Returns and allowances	2	
3	Subtract line 2 from line 1	3	
4	Cost of goods sold (from line 42 on page 2)	4	
5	**Gross profit.** Subtract line 4 from line 3	5	
6	Other income, including Federal and state gasoline or fuel tax credit or refund (see page C-3)	6	
7	**Gross income.** Add lines 5 and 6 ▶	7	

Appendix 10-1. IRS Schedule C

(2 of 4)

Part II **Expenses.** Enter expenses for business use of your home **only** on line 30.

Line	Description	Box	Amount	Line	Description	Box	Amount
8	Advertising	8		19	Pension and profit-sharing plans	19	
9	Bad debts from sales or services (see page C-3)	9		20	Rent or lease (see page C-4):		
				a	Vehicles, machinery, and equipment	20a	
10	Car and truck expenses (see page C-3)	10		b	Other business property	20b	
11	Commissions and fees	11		21	Repairs and maintenance	21	
12	Depletion	12		22	Supplies (not included in Part III)	22	
				23	Taxes and licenses	23	
13	Depreciation and section 179 expense deduction (not included in Part III) (see page C-3)	13		24	Travel, meals, and entertainment:		
				a	Travel	24a	
14	Employee benefit programs (other than on line 19)	14		b	Meals and entertainment		
15	Insurance (other than health)	15		c	Enter nondeductible amount included on line 24b (see page C-5)		
16	Interest:						
a	Mortgage (paid to banks, etc.)	16a		d	Subtract line 24c from line 24b	24d	
b	Other	16b		25	Utilities	25	
17	Legal and professional services	17		26	Wages (less employment credits)	26	
18	Office expense	18		27	Other expenses (from line 48 on page 2)	27	

28 **Total expenses** before expenses for business use of home. Add lines 8 through 27 in columns ▶ 28

29 Tentative profit (loss). Subtract line 28 from line 7 . . . 29

30 Expenses for business use of your home. Attach **Form 8829** . . . 30

31 **Net profit or (loss).** Subtract line 30 from line 29.
- If a profit, enter on **Form 1040, line 12,** and ALSO on **Schedule SE, line 2** (statutory employees, see page C-6). Estates and trusts, enter on Form 1041, line 3.
- If a loss, you MUST go on to line 32.

} 31

32 If you have a loss, check the box that describes your investment in this activity (see page C-6).
- If you checked 32a, enter the loss on **Form 1040, line 12,** and ALSO on **Schedule SE, line 2** (statutory employees, see page C-6). Estates and trusts, enter on Form 1041, line 3.
- If you checked 32b, you MUST attach **Form 6198.**

} 32a ☐ All investment is at risk.
32b ☐ Some investment is not at risk.

For Paperwork Reduction Act Notice, see Form 1040 instructions. Cat. No. 11334P **Schedule C (Form 1040) 1999**

Appendix 10-1. IRS Schedule C
(3 of 4)

Schedule C (Form 1040) 1999 Page 2

Part III **Cost of Goods Sold** (see page C-6)

33	Method(s) used to value closing inventory: a ☐ Cost b ☐ Lower of cost or market c ☐ Other (attach explanation)		
34	Was there any change in determining quantities, costs, or valuations between opening and closing inventory? If "Yes," attach explanation . . . ☐ Yes ☐ No		
35	Inventory at beginning of year. If different from last year's closing inventory, attach explanation . .	35	
36	Purchases less cost of items withdrawn for personal use . . .	36	
37	Cost of labor. Do not include any amounts paid to yourself . . .	37	
38	Materials and supplies . . .	38	
39	Other costs . . .	39	
40	Add lines 35 through 39 . . .	40	
41	Inventory at end of year . . .	41	
42	**Cost of goods sold.** Subtract line 41 from line 40. Enter the result here and on page 1, line 4 . .	42	

Appendix 10-1. IRS Schedule C

(4 of 4)

Part IV **Information on Your Vehicle.** Complete this part **ONLY** if you are claiming car or truck expenses on line 10 and are not required to file Form 4562 for this business. See the instructions for line 13 on page C-3 to find out if you must file.

43 When did you place your vehicle in service for business purposes? (month, day, year) ▶ ..../......../....... .

44 Of the total number of miles you drove your vehicle during 1999, enter the number of miles you used your vehicle for:

a Business .... b Commuting .... c Other ....

45 Do you (or your spouse) have another vehicle available for personal use? . . . . ☐ Yes ☐ No

46 Was your vehicle available for use during off-duty hours? . . . . ☐ Yes ☐ No

47a Do you have evidence to support your deduction? . . . . ☐ Yes ☐ No

b If "Yes," is the evidence written? . . . . ☐ Yes ☐ No

Part V **Other Expenses.** List below business expenses not included on lines 8–26 or line 30.

48 **Total other expenses.** Enter here and on page 1, line 27 48	

Schedule C (Form 1040) 1999

Chapter 11

Liability and How to Minimize It

As always happens in these cases, the fault was attributed to me, the engineer, as though I had not taken all precautions to ensure the success of the work. What could I have done better? (Written 152 A.D. by Nonius Datus, the Roman engineer responsible for the design and construction of a water supply tunnel through a mountain in what is now Algeria, upon visiting the construction site at which the tunnel was being excavated from both ends. He had just learned that the segments were out of alignment and had passed each other. As quoted in de Camp, 1963, p. 27)

BACKGROUND

Engineers should not practice law just as lawyers should not practice engineering. However, just as knowing the basics of business accounting helps the sole proprietor conduct his or her business, so knowing the basics of law will help the sole proprietor minimize liability. Individual practitioners should know enough about the legal aspects of engineering practice to recognize when they need to take certain actions or to know when legal counsel would be prudent. The purpose of this chapter is to provide you, as a potential sole proprietor, with an understanding of basic legal principles and broad guidelines of law.

After citing examples of circumstances in which the sole proprietor should know some legal fundamentals, selected legal terms are explained. Three ways in which liability is incurred are introduced. Ways to minimize liability are discussed and this chapter concludes with an admonition to keep liability minimization in perspective.

THE SOLE PROPRIETOR AND LEGAL CONSIDERATIONS

Dunham et al (1979, Chapter 1) discusses ways and describe situations in which a free lancer may need to know basic principles and broad guidelines of law. Supplementing these with additional circumstances leads to the seven items summarized here.

1. **Preparing contracts for services**: The individual practitioner may need to prepare or, more likely, help to prepare a contract or agreement for services between him or her and various entities such as a consulting engineering firm, a construction contractor, or a manufacturer.

2. **Interpretation of contracts once a project is underway**: Even a well-crafted, mutually acceptable contract or agreement will require numerous interpretations during the project. For example, the client's representative may call the individual practitioner, after reviewing a draft design, and request that more alternatives be developed and examined. The sole proprietor must decide if the request is reasonable, that is, within or beyond the scope of the contract.

3. **Managing to minimize personal and organizational liability**: As individual practitioners go about their work, especially when doing what may appear to be relatively mundane operations and tasks, they should be aware of ways in which liability is minimized. Numerous suggestions, many of which are both simple and powerful, are presented later in this chapter.

4. **Anticipating or preparing for expert witness testimony**: This situation is similar to the preceding, but much more focused. It assumes the sole proprietor is going to be involved as an expert witness within the litigation process. Expert witness testimony is not treated in this chapter, but is discussed elsewhere (e.g., McQuillan, 1984).

5. **Being aware of the requirements in local, state, and federal laws and rules**: The practice of engineering, and some other technical professions, in the public and private sector, is typically heavily influenced and constrained by the requirements of local, state, and federal laws and administrative rules. You are strongly

urged to learn about those requirements in the very early stages of a project.

Assume, for example, that you are retained to plan and design the stormwater management system for a new residential development on the periphery of a growing U.S. city. The community is likely to have zoning, subdivision, drainage, and other codes and requirements that must be satisfied by your project. County and regional rules and regulations may also apply particularly if the development will initially be outside of the corporate limits of the city. State water laws may also be applicable. For example, if the stormwater system includes a detention facility, the outlet control structure may qualify as a dam under state law and require a state permit. Federal regulations and codes may also apply. Perhaps a stream passing through the area has a 100-year flood plain delineated under the flood insurance program administered by the Federal Emergency Management Agency (FEMA). A stormwater discharge permit may be required under the National Pollution Discharge Elimination System (NPDES).

Note that all of the preceding examples apply only to the water resources portion of the project. A similar set of city, county, regional, state, and federal expectations may also exist for other aspects of the new development such as its wastewater system, its water supply system, and its streets and highways. Unfortunately, too many technical professionals, many of whom should know better, tend to move well into a planning or design project before determining the applicable rules and regulations.

6. **Being aware of the ways in which state, federal, and other programs may provide funding for clients' projects**: While local through federal regulations and legislation may sometimes be viewed as a problem because of the many requirements that must be met, some legislation, particularly at the state and federal level, also includes a "carrot" in the form of partial funding. The sole proprietor, striving for full service, will commit the necessary resources to be aware of existing legislation that could be useful to clients.

   For example, some states have legislation which enables local communities to implement stormwater management utilities. These utilities provide, through user and other fees, a means of equitably generating revenue to finance the planning, design, construction, operation and maintenance of stormwater systems. Individual practitioners should know about such legislation and how to help a given community establish a utility.

7. **Being aware of relevant pending legislation and possible impacts on projects**: In addition to knowing about already enacted legislation, you should be tracking pending legislation. Given the multi-year span of some planning-design-construction or manufacturing projects, legislation being debated at the beginning of the process might be enacted and available to benefit a client near the end of the process.

LEGAL TERMINOLOGY

The legal profession, like the engineering, medical, and many other professions, has a special set of terminology. Selected legal terms are defined in FIGURE 11-1. The four most

BREACH: "Violation of a right, a duty or a law, either by an act of commission or by nonfulfillment of an obligation."[d]

CAVEAT EMPTOR: "Let the buyer beware…the buyer should take pains to discover for himself any obvious defects in an article he is about to purchase."[d]

CONTRACTOR: "...the party (either individual or organization) who undertakes for a stated price to supply goods or to perform a construction job or other project for the owner...controls the work of construction…"[a]

DRAWINGS: "...sketches and line drawings as well as...notes of explanation or instruction inserted thereon. Prints and other reproductions of drawings are generally deemed to be the equivalent of the originals from which they are made."[a]

ENGINEER: "...the architect or the engineer (or both) who acts for and in behalf of the owner...an engineering organization as well as an individual."[a]

FRAUD: "Intentionally deceitful practice aimed at depriving another person of his rights or doing him injury in some respect."[d]

INJUNCTION: "A writ issued by a court of equity ordering a person to refrain from a given course of action."[d]

Figure 11-1. Definitions of selected legal terms. (1 of 3)

LAW, COMMON: "...those maxims and doctrines which have their origin in court decisions and are not founded upon statute."[b]

LAW, STATUTE: "...rule of conduct, enacted by the duly authorized legislative authority...represents the express, written will of the lawmaking power..."[b]

LIABILITY: Being bound or obligated according to law or equity.

LITIGIOUS: Prone to engage in law suits.

NEGLIGENCE: "...breaches...duty to exercise requisite care and expertise...below the appropriate standard of care."[d]

OWNER: "...individual or organization for whom something is to be built or furnished under contract...the purchaser who pays for the goods or services."[a]

PRIVITY: "Successive (or mutual) relationship to the same property rights; a connection between parties."[d]

STATUTES OF LIMITATIONS: "...apply to architect-engineers and construction contractors and establish time beyond which these parties are no longer liable for damages arising out of completed construction projects...a typical statute provides for a three-year period for torts (negligence) and a six-year period for breach of contract."[e]

Figure 11-1. Definitions of selected legal terms. (2 of 3)

TORT: "essentially, 'tort' is very similar to 'wrong'; yet the former term is not intended to include any and all wrongful acts done by one person to the detriment of another but only those for which the victim may demand legal redress. Torts may be committed intentionally or unintentionally and with or without force. At the risk of oversimplification it may be said that tortious acts consist of the unprivileged commission (or omission, as the case may be) or acts whereby another individual receives an injury to his person, property, or reputation. A tort is distinguished from a crime in that the former is a private injury on account of which suit may be brought by the affected party, while the latter is an offense against the public for which any retribution must be sought by the appropriate governmental authority. Obviously, it is entirely possible for a single act to constitute at once a tort and a crime."[c] (Note: Key ideas - wrongful act against a person or his property or reputation, intentional or unintentional, victim seeks legal remedy.)

WRITTEN INFORMATION: "...information typed or printed or recorded in longhand."[a]

---

a) Dunham et al, 1979, Chapter 1 - "Introduction"
b) Dunham et al, 1979, Chapter 2 - "Law and Courts"
c) Dunham et al, 1979, Chapter 20 - "Torts"
d) Dunham et al, 1979, Chapter 25 - "Professional Liability of Architects and Engineers."

Preceding quotes with permission of McGraw-Hill Companies.

e) Clough, 1986, Chapter 4 - "Drawings and Specifications"

Figure 11-1. Definitions of selected legal terms. (3 of 3)

important terms in FIGURE 11-1 for the free lancer are "breach," "fraud," "negligence," and "liability." Breach, fraud and negligence are the three ways in which an individual professional can incur liability. Each of these terms is discussed later in this chapter.

CHANGING ATTITUDES: ADDED BURDEN ON THE PROFESSIONAL

Decades ago, in the U.S. and elsewhere, people were inclined to take risks and accept the consequences whether they were favorable or unfavorable. However, in recent times citizens of many countries have become increasingly inclined to seek relief through legal means, especially when risk taking has resulted in unfavorable consequences.

A new concept of social justice has evolved. As in the past, accidents and failures are recognized as being expensive as a result of factors such as medical costs, materials, and schedule delays. However, increasingly common is the idea that someone else should pay the costs, or at least part of them. More specifically, the tendency is to look for "deep pockets," that is, those individuals, organizations, or other entities having the greatest financial resources which, depending on the situation, may be a government agency, a contractor, a consulting engineer, a manufacturing firm, or you—an individual practitioner. In effect, there has been a litigation explosion across much of society and this includes the engineering field (Allen, 1988). As stated by DPIC (1988, p. vii) "...in this (litigious) environment, the private practice of a design professional can be particularly vulnerable, because of the damage that even an unfounded lawsuit can do to a reputation and financial stability." Forewarned is truly forearmed in minimizing exposure to litigation. An unfortunate result of the litigation explosion is the tendency to stifle innovation within engineering practice (Huber, 1988).

LIABILITY: INCURRING IT

As indicated in FIGURE 11-1, liability is defined as "Being bound or obligated according to the law or equity." Liability means that an individual or an organization is responsible for doing a conscientious job and, if they do not, they will be held accountable. The concept of liability and its incorporation into laws goes back to ancient times. For example, 4000 years ago the Babylonians developed the Code of Hammurabi which clearly stated the importance of individual responsibility. As quoted in Petroski (1985, pp. 34), the Code included these house-building provisions:

> *If a builder build a house for a man and do not make its construction firm, and the house which he has built collapse and cause the death of the owner of the house that builder shall be put to death. If it cause the death of the son of the owner of the house, they shall put to death a son of that builder. If it cause the death of a slave of the owner of the house, he shall give to the owner of the house a slave of equal value. If it destroy property, he shall restore whatever it destroyed, and because he did not make the house which he built firm and it collapsed, he shall rebuild the house which collapsed from his own property. If a builder build a house for a man and do not make its construction meet the requirements and a wall fall in, that builder shall strengthen the wall at his own expense.*

As quoted in Biswas (1970, p. 20), this dam maintenance requirement was part of the Code:

If any one be too lazy to keep his dam in proper condition, and does not keep it so; if then the dam breaks and all the fields are flooded, then shall he whose dam the break occurred be sold for money and the money shall replace the corn which he has caused to be ruined.

These 4000 year old texts nicely illustrate the concept of liability, that is being held accountable for one's actions. The texts are also notable for the absence of ambiguity.

Unfortunately, there are many and varied ways in which today's individual practitioner can incur liability (e.g., Clough 1986, Chapter 4; Dunham et al, 1979, Chapter 25). One way to illustrate the potential liability exposure of a sole proprietor is to enumerate some of the services typically provided by him or her and then think through some of the possible related liabilities. This approach was used to construct FIGURE 11-2 which lists 18 types of services that could be provided by an individual practitioner and, for most of them, gives examples of potential liability in terms of fraud, breach of contract, and negligence. Recall that fraud, breach, and negligence are defined in FIGURE 11-1. As suggested by FIGURE 11-2, liability-incurring opportunities abound in the practice of engineering and related technical professions.

To elaborate, ***breach*** has little or nothing to do with intention, but nevertheless consists of violating a right, a duty, or a law. Simply failing to deliver plans and specifications on time, as specified in a contract or agreement could constitute breach. ***Fraud***, which is intentional, and deceitful, is illustrated by billing a client for products not delivered or falsely stating that a necessary government permit had been secured.

1. Participating in necessary conferences and preliminary studies.

   Breach: contract promised X meetings, only had Y.

2. Interpreting physical restrictions as to the use of the land.

   Negligence: failed to allow for building setbacks.

3. Examining the site of the construction.

4. Preparing and/or interpreting soil, subsoil, and hydrologic data.

5. Preparing drawings or verifying and interpreting existing drawings or construction.

   Negligence: proposed water main conflicts with natural gas line.

   Breach: drawings late.

6. Assisting in procuring of financing for the project.

   Fraud: A/E "steers" client to certain lender in return for kickback from lender.

Figure 11-2. Services which may be provided by an individual practitioner and possible related liabilities. (1 of 3)

7. Assisting in presentation of a project before bodies possessing approval-disapproval power.

   Fraud: falsely claim that lower level government units and agencies approve.

8. Preparing drawings and specifications for architectural, structural, plumbing, heating, electrical, and other mechanical work.

   Negligence: inadequate thermal insulation leads to fire.

9. Assisting in the drafting of proposals and contracts.

10. Preparing cost estimates.

    Negligence: numerical error.

11. Obtaining bid from contractors.

    Fraud: alter a bid to favor a contractor.

12. Letting contracts with owner's written approval.

13. Inspecting the contractor's work on regular basis, including the checking of shop drawings (but without dictating the method or means by which the contractor seeks to accomplish the desired results).

    Negligence: failing to note an unsatisfactory change (e.g., 1981 Kansas City Hyatt failure.)

Figure 11-2. Services which may be provided by an individual practitioner and possible related liabilities. (2 of 3)

14. Interpreting for the contractor the meaning of the drawings and specifications.

15. Ordering the correction or removal of all work and materials not in strict conformity with specifications.

16. Keeping accurate books and records.

    Breach: failing to do and submit when required.

17. Preparing as-built drawings which show construction changes and final locations of mechanical and electrical lines.

    Negligence: incorrectly locating buried electric line leading to later disastrous excavation accident.

18. Issuing certificates of payment.

    Negligence: failing to verify work was performed.

Figure 11-2. Services which may be provided by an individual practitioner and possible related liabilities. (3 of 3)

(Source: List (the 18 points) quoted from Dunham et al., 1979, pp. 426-427. Reproduced with permission of McGraw-Hill Companies. Examples of liabilities were added.)

Negligence, the most common of the three ways in which technical professionals and their organizations incur liability, means failing to exercise care and provide expertise in accordance with the standard of the profession. For example, calculation error is likely to be considered negligence. You, as an individual practitioner, must recognize that being honest and well-intentioned are simply not enough in avoiding negligence. You must be disciplined in the manner in which you provide services if negligence and the resulting liability are to be avoided.

You are not expected to be perfect (Dunham et al, 1979, p. 427). Clients contract for service, not insurance. Engineering and similar organizations cannot guarantee perfect plans and specifications or flawless products. Perfection is not expected of the technical professional. However, the professional is obligated to "...exercise ordinary professional skill and diligence and to conform to accepted...standards" (Dunham et al, 1979, p. 427).

LIABILITY: LEARNING FROM FAILURES

> *The only thing new in the world is the history you don't know.* (President Harry S. Truman quoted by Miller [1974, p. 21])

A review of some actual failures and the resulting death, disruption, economic loss, and other consequences provides insight into the cause of the failures and the related liabilities. Although liability can be incurred as a result of breach, fraud, and negligence, an examination of failures supports the thesis that negligence is by far the dominant cause. You should become a student of failures, especially if your services include structural design. For a review of selected failures and lessons learned from them, refer to Chapter 10, "Legal Framework" in Walesh (1995).

LIABILITY: MINIMIZING IT

As noted at the beginning of this chapter, society is becoming more litigious, that is, more likely to take legal action. Therefore, sole proprietors must be even more diligent in taking preventive and remedial action.

Insurance: Financial Protection

While purchasing liability insurance won't directly prevent lawsuits being brought against an individual practitioner, the availability of the insurance will provide some financial protection if a liability action is initiated. The insurer, in exchange for regular premium payments, agrees to make liability payments and defend suits arising out of negligence or alleged negligence in the provision of professional services by the insured.

As with most insurance policies there are exclusions, that is, actions and activities that are not covered by liability insurance. Examples are the failure of the insured to complete services on time, intentional fraudulent and other acts of the insured, and the insured providing services outside of the insurer's area of expertise (Dunham et al, 1979, p.452). As is also the case with some other forms of insurance, professional liability insurance typically has deductible provisions, that is, an initial amount of loss that is not covered by the insurance.

Liability insurance is expensive when annual premiums are quantified, for example, as a percent of annual billings for a sole proprietor. Liability insurance premiums are of the same order of magnitude as the after-tax profit of many consulting engineering firms. Premiums tend to be higher for greater risk areas of service such as structural design. Incidentally, insurance premiums are part of overhead and, therefore, go right to the bottom line on the sole proprietor's income statement. There was a trend in the last decade for liability insurance premiums, measured as a percent of gross annual revenue, to diminish apparently reflecting improved management of risk and liability exposure by consulting engineering firms (ACE, 1999).

You should know that not all consulting firms purchase liability insurance in that some "go bare." For example, a 1998-99 liability survey by the ACEC based on responses from 622 consulting engineering firms revealed that 6% had no liability insurance (ACE, 1999). Small firms are much more likely to go without liability insurance than large firms. Firms without liability insurance are, in effect, self-insured. Parsons (1999) offers advice on obtaining liability insurance.

If you think that liability insurance is appropriate for your intended practice, many sources are available. Many professional liability insurance carriers are listed below, based largely on information from the National Society of Professional Engineers (NSPE, December, 1999). Not all of the carriers will necessarily serve sole proprietors.

- American Equity Insurance Company

  Tel: 630-916-0500
  Fax: 630-916-0555
  Professional Underwriters Agency, Inc.
  Two Trans Am Plaza, Suite 330
  Oak Brook Terrace, IL 60181-4291

- American Society of Civil Engineers, Professional Liability Insurance Plan

  http://www.asce.org
  Tel: 800-435-7931
  1801 Alexander Bell Dr.
  Reston, VA 20191-4400

- Benchmark Professional Insurance Services, Inc.
  Email: bpisil@aol.com
  Tel: 630-986-5151
  Fax: 630-986-9780
  201 East Ogden Avenue, Suite 212
  Hinsdale, IL 60521-3633

- CNA – Victor O. Schinnerer & Co., Inc.
  http://www.schinnerer.com
  Tel: 301-961-9800
  Fax: 301-951-5444
  Two Wisconsin Circle
  Chevy Chase, MD 20815-7003

- DPIC (Design Professionals Insurance Company) Companies
  http://www.dpic.com/
  Tel: 800-227-4284
  Fax: 831-649-1734
  P. O. Box DPIC
  Monterey, CA 93940

- Gulf Insurance Company
  Email: bpisil@aol.com
  Tel: 630-986-5151
  Fax: 630-986-9780
  Benchmark Professional Insurance Services, Inc.
  201 East Ogden Avenue, Suite 212
  Hinsdale, IL 60521-3633

- Kemper Professional Liability
  Tel: 877-237-6588
  Fax: 410-872-8180
  8830 Stanford Blvd., Suite 200
  Columbia, MD 20145

- Lexington Insurance Company
  Tel: 617-330-8266
  Fax: 617-439-9794
  200 State Street
  Boston, MA 02109

- Lloyd's AVRECO, Inc.
  Tel: 312-346-6161
  Fax: 312-580-0106
  10 S. LaSalle Street, 12th Floor
  Chicago, IL 60603

- Lloyd's of London, Illinois R.B. Jones, Inc.
  Tel: 888-957-0505
  Tel: 248-538-1379
  Fax: 248-538-1385
  220 Kaufman Financial Center
  30833 Northwestern Highway
  Farmington Hills, MI 48334

- RA&MCO Insurance Services, Underwriters at Lloyd's and certain London companies, Insurance Company of the West
  http://www.ramco-ins.com
  Tel: 800-684-7475
  Tel: 925-685-1600
  Fax: 925-685-1750
  2300 Clayton Road, Suite 600
  Concord, CA 94520

- Reliance, Reliance National

  http://www.reliancenational.com
  Tel: 212-858-9689
  Fax: 212-858-8788
  77 Water Street
  New York, NY 10005

- SAFECO Insurance Co., Insight Insurance Services, Inc.

  http://www.insightinsurance.com
  Tel: 800-447-4626
  Fax: 630-505-1221
  4225 Naperville Road, Suite 265
  Lisle, IL 60532-3633

- United Capital Insurance Co., Olympic Underwriting Managers, Inc.

  Tel: 312-922-8800
  Fax: 312-294-9621
  311 South Wacker Drive, Suite 500
  Chicago, IL 60606

- Zurich-American Insurance Group

  http://www.zurichus.com
  Tel: 312-419-7491
  Fax: 312-419-4666
  200 W. Adams, Suite 1800
  Chicago, IL 60606

While on the subject of insurance, consider other types of insurance that may be appropriate for your sole proprietorship (Lindeburg, 1997, pp. 33-34). For example, you may want general liability insurance because of your responsibility for the physical safety of people visiting or working in your office. A fire insurance policy will be needed if you own your office or office building. Comprehensive insurance may be advisable if you are concerned about crimes such as burglary and forged checks.

Preventive Actions

While liability insurance, which provides some financial protection in case of liability litigation, may be considered optional by a sole proprietor, he or she should aggressively and systematically undertake programs to minimize liability, particularly that which may be incurred as a result of negligence. FIGURE 11-3, lists 15 ways to reduce liability, each of which is discussed here. All of the listed ways to reduce liability are potentially applicable to the individual practitioner.

1. **Incorporate practice**: This may limit the sole proprietor's liability to the corporation's assets. It will require officers.

2. **Limit practice to "safer" disciplines**: Examples of high litigation-potential areas of service are poorly financed developers, roofing projects, structural designs, hazardous waste, geotechnical, and construction inspection. A variation on this liability reduction approach is to sub-contract areas of service having higher litigation potential (Brown, 1988; Vansant, 1982).

3. **Maintain currency and competence**: A proactive program of formal and informal activities is needed to maintain your currency and competence. As discussed earlier and stated in FIGURE 11-1, technical services that fall below the appropriate "standard of care" may be deemed negligent and result in liability. Your best interests require that you

1. Incorporate practice.
2. Limit practice to "safer" disciplines.
3. Maintain currency and competence.
4. Use standard contract forms.
5. Utilize tested legal language.
6. Document everything.
7. Supplement written documentation with photographs, slides, and video tape.
8. Accept primary responsibility for use of computer programs and models.
9. Separate facts and opinions.
10. Hire only insured sub-consultants.
11. Respond in a timely fashion.
12. Use peer review.
13. Do it right the first time!
14. Communicate-communicate-communicate with those you serve.
15. Place liability-limiting provisions in contracts.

Figure 11-3. 15 ways to reduce an individual practitioner's liability.

remain current and competent in your areas of technical specialization. Clearly, being current and competent includes understanding of legal principles, with emphasis on liability, as set forth in this chapter.

4. **Use standard contract forms**: Consider using standard contract forms such as those produced by the Engineers Joint Contract Document Committee for use by firms and constructors. Committee members are the ACEC (www.acec.org), the ASCE (www.asce.org), and the NSPE (http://www.nspe.org/). Davis (1986) lists many advantages of such forms including the all important periodic and cooperative review of the forms by organizations representing all interests.

5. **Utilize tested legal language**: Consider use of tested legal language in contracts and agreements. Certain words and phrases, even when and perhaps especially when well-intended, can lead to contract conflict and even claims of negligence or even breach of contract or fraud. Hayden (1987) effectively presents some commonly used words and phases to avoid and he offers suggested and safer replacements. Hayden's contribution is presented in FIGURE 11-4. According to Brown (1991), "...the big print giveth and small print taketh away." In other words, contracts and agreements, and the proposals used to obtain them, should be written and read very carefully.

6. **Document everything**: Everything means essentially everything, including, but not limited to, meetings, telephone calls, field reconnaissance, and conversations. The idea is to assume that everything

Do Not Use	Example Replacements
All existing information will be gathered	Readily available information will be reviewed and collected as needed
Coordination performed ***at all times***.	Client will be apprised of approval progress
Highly trained professionals	Professionals
Prepare summaries of ***all*** meetings	Prepare summaries of monthly project status meetings with client
Close coordination of ***all stages*** of the work	Perform interdisciplinary milestone review at 15%, 30%, 60% and 90%
All required professional support	The work will be performed by our staff
Will ***complete all*** project services	Will prepare and submit for review and approval normal engineering drawings suitable for construction
Is ***exceptionally*** well qualified	For this opportunity we are qualified because

Figure 11-4. Expressions to use and not to use in contracts and agreements. (1 of 3)

High quality reports	Our reports will be suitable for
Only the best	Staff selected will be appropriate for the work assigned
The ***highest level*** of quality	The work performed will satisfy contract requirements
Guarantee ***successful*** project completion	Committed to perform as contracted for scope, schedule and budget
Only experienced and qualified staff will be assigned	Technical staff will be assigned as appropriate
As necessary	Not less than once per
At ***all*** times	Will be done less than once per
Or approved equal	Similar in our opinion as to function
Insure; ensure; assure	Reasonable effort will be made

Figure 11-4. Expressions to use and not to use in contracts and agreements. (2 of 3)

Maximum	Not less than two per month
Minimum	Not more than two per month
Periodically	Not less than once per
Supervise; inspect	Observe and report
Certify; warrant; guarantee	Statement as to our judgement based on

Figure 11-4. Expressions to use and not to use in contracts and agreements. (3 of 3)

(Source: Adapted with permission from Hayden, 1987.)

will someday be viewed by your peers or, worse yet, by opponents in litigation (MacLean, 1982; Vansant, 1982; Vansant, 1983). You should have a uniform documentation system consisting of components such as standard filing procedures, special forms, and a project management system.

7. **Supplement written documentation with photographs, slides, and video tape**: Images are an extremely effective form of communication and, therefore, documentation.

8. **Accept primary responsibility for use of computer programs and models:** You have the primary responsibility for the correctness of computer programs or models used in your projects and for the appropriateness of the uses. Even if the software contains errors, the professional using the program or model, that is, you, not the outside model developer, is likely to carry all or most of the liability if a problem arises (Backman, 1993; ENR, October 28, 1991; Mishkin and Schwartz, 1990). Because heavy use is made of computer programs and models in technical environments, this liability principle should be understood.

9. **Separate facts and opinions:** When preparing memoranda, letters, reports, and other forms of documentation, clearly indicate when data are being presented and when opinions are being expressed (Vansant, 1982).

10. **Hire only insured sub-consultants**: This practice will tend to limit your liability because the sub-consultant's liability insurance will be available.

Brown (1988) notes that another, and sometimes preferable alternative, is to have sub-consultants contract directly with the owner.

11. **Respond in a timely fashion**: Requests from clients or customers and from sub-contractors for data, information, or decisions should receive a timely response. To do otherwise is to risk a subsequent charge of negligence (MacLean, 1982).

12. **Use peer review**: The idea is to have your technical work reviewed by one or more peers who, at the outset, are not familiar with the project, but are experts in the disciplines represented by the project. Diminished probability of errors and omissions is the obvious advantage of peer review. Potential problems or challenges inherent in peer review include increased design costs, interpersonal conflict between reviewers and reviewees, and expanding the number of potential liable individuals or organizations if a failure occurs (Preziosi, 1988; Vansant, 1982).

13. **Do it right the first time!**: MacLean (1982) notes that by doing projects right the first time, not only are time and money saved in the long run for the sole proprietor, but last-minute rushing and the inevitable errors resulting in liability exposure are reduced. Recall the earlier advice to plan your work and then work your plan.

14. **Communicate-communicate-communicate with those you serve**: All legal and other technicalities aside, there must be a clear understanding of expectations prior to formalization of an agreement

between an individual proprietor and a client or customer. Failure to achieve a "meeting of the minds" sows the seeds of conflict and litigation. Once a project is underway, ongoing communication is essential with the primary responsibility for the effectiveness of that communication lying with you. Client and customer communication is important from a liability minimization perspective because current clients and customers—not third parties—are probably the principal source of liability for an engineering organization. Miller (1987) cites the mid-1980's experience of CH2M HILL, a large multi-discipline consulting engineering firm. He states that "...65% of the significant claims and 85% of the monetary liability attributable to such claims were brought by dissatisfied clients, not by third parties or members of the public."

15. **Place liability-limiting provisions in contracts:** Possibilities include aggregate limits on liability, and limiting potential liability to amounts recoverable with the sole proprietor's liability insurance (Brown, 1988).

Danger Signals

Andrews and Ruzzo (1988) identify some client or client/related behaviors or circumstances which may indicate that serious legal problems are imminent. Examples include a reduction in the frequency of client or customer contact and a change toward the negative in the tone of such contact; involvement of new third parties including potential plaintiffs and their attorneys; exclusion from project-related meetings and communications; or customer complaints to third parties about your organization; and termination of your services by the client or customer. If you think you sense client or customer dissatisfaction, immediately take action. Then the situation can be analyzed and, if a problem exists, corrective actions or at least damage control, can be taken.

MAINTAINING PERSPECTIVE ON LIABILITY MINIMIZATION

Much of what is done by an individual practitioner to minimize liability exposure is also being done for one or more other reasons, some of which may even be more important—this is just good management. You should guard against letting the "tail wag the dog," that is, becoming overly fearful, if not paranoid, about liability. For example, peer review, which is presented as one way of minimizing liability, is also likely to yield a more cost-effective design as measured by life-cycle costs. Documentation, another liability minimization device, is also very useful in planning a project; coordinating a project; writing a report on a project; as a guide for future, similar projects; and as a resource for "surprise" meetings. While timely response to client requests will surely minimize liability exposure, it is also a mark of good service. Use of standard, tested contract and agreement language, is another liability minimization measure, and also a time-saving device.

REVIEW

In closing this chapter titled "Liability and How to Minimize It," reflect on the key ideas. The sole proprietor should know basic principles of law because those principles are present in so much that he or she does. Liability is defined as being bound or obligated by law or equity. You, as an individual practitioner, can incur liability by breach, fraud or negligence. The last, negligence, is the most likely. Financial protection against liability is provided by liability insurance. Liability exposure can be minimized by working smart. Fifteen specific suggestions are presented.

Having offered advice on minimizing liability, consider this statement:

> *The greatest mistake you can make in life is to be continually fearing you will make one.* (E. Hubbard)

Chapter 12

What if You "Fail"?

> *You miss 100% of the shots you never take.* (Wayne Gretzky)

RISKING FAILURE

Success as a sole proprietor entails risking failure, financial and otherwise. The individual proprietor isn't risk averse. Risk taking is part of the price of real achievement, that is, of realizing one's unique potential and of making significant contributions. Risk is a reality and, like other elements of an individual practitioner's business, it must be managed. Ralph Waldo Emerson (1936, p. 32) in his essay "Self Reliance," wrote this about the role of risk in realizing one's potential:

> *There is a time in every man's education when he arrives at the conviction that envy is ignorance; that imitation is suicide; that he must take himself for better, for worse, as his portion; that though the wide universe is full of good, no kernel of nourishing corn can come to him but through his toil bestowed on that plot of ground which is*

given to him to till. The power which resides in him is new in nature, and none but he knows what that is which he can do, nor does he know until he has tried... God will not have his work made manifest by cowards.

Presented in this chapter are thoughts on the possibility of failing as an individual practitioner, types of failure, and consequences of failure.

DON'T GIVE UP TOO SOON

Don't expect to be successful as a sole proprietor without hard work. As someone anonymously said, "The dictionary is the only place where success comes before work." Don't expect to be successful as an individual practitioner without overcoming setbacks. As someone else anonymously said, "setbacks pave the way for comebacks." What you view as failure may be a setback, a restart, or another tack in a series of tacks. Emerson (1936, p. 40), in his essay "Self Reliance" also reminds us that "The voyage of the best ship is a zigzag of a hundred tacks." Make sure you have the ***GUTS***, that is don't ***G***ive ***U***p ***T***oo ***S***oon.

CALLING IT QUITS

You've decided to "call it quits." You worked smart, hard, long and with integrity. However, no matter how patiently, optimistically, or creatively you look at it, your sole proprietorship has failed or is about to. You know it, you do not want to take another run at being an individual practitioner—at least not now!

VIEW FROM THE PROSPECTIVE EMPLOYER'S SIDE

You want and need to get back into an employee situation. You need the income, benefits and "security," at least for a while. You are concerned that your unsuccessful sole proprietorship will hamper your re-entry into the employment market. Guess what? You will "jump" to the top of the list of candidates. Why? Put on your "employee-hiring hat." Chances are, you've worn this hat in one or more organizations. You have screened resumes, interviewed candidates, and hired and coached employees. Which of the following people would you be inclined to learn more about, interview, and probably hire?

1. Worked for one public organization.
2. Worked for one business organization.
3. Worked for one public and one business organization.
4. Worked for one or more public and one or more business organizations.
5. Worked for one or more public and one or more business organizations and "failed" as a sole proprietor.
6. Worked for one or more public and one or more business organizations and succeeded as a sole proprietor.

Get the idea? The preceding are listed in order of increasing desirability. Variety and richness of one's experience increases value, even if interspersed with "failure." While we learn when we succeed, we also learn when we fail. In fact, those who "shoot low" and "succeed," probably learn much less then those who "shoot high" and "fail." Put on your employer "hat." Whom do you want on your team? Someone who, if he or she "shot" at all, "shot low" and made it, or someone who "shot high," and sometimes "missed?"

THE WORST KINDS OF FAILURE

Although it may sound like an oxymoron and be less than comforting, there are "good failures" as suggested by the preceding discussion. There are also "bad failures." That is, some failure modes would be very detrimental if not fatal to your continuation as a sole proprietor and to your re-entry into the employment market. Consider three likely fatal failure modes.

- The first of these is to have failed as an individual practitioner because of unethical practices. Unshielded by being a member of a larger organization, your unethical practices are much more likely to be widely known and associated specifically with you.

- A second type of fatal failure is to be found liable for errors and omissions. Again, the focus will be solely on you as the sole proprietor. Contrast this with an errors and omission finding against an engineering organization where the "blame" may be "spread around."

- A third type of likely fatal failure as an individual practitioner, is to have "earned" a reputation for not delivering. Missing schedules, exceeding budgets, and failing to provide all deliverables are examples.

The preceding three types of fatal failures are certainly not unique to sole proprietorships. However, when they occur in the sole proprietorship, 100% of the negative consequences are likely to be associated with the sole proprietor. Avoiding fatal failures in a sole proprietorship requires the same kinds of diligence needed to avoid them in a typical engineering organization, namely, disciplined, conscientious, and competent efforts.

Individuals who have the courage to set out on their own; work hard, long, and with integrity; and yet do not succeed as individual practitioners might be considered to have experienced a "good" failure. On the failure scale, such a failure is far from that experienced by the individual who, having the courage to start an individual practice, let that effort be undermined by carelessness, incompetence, unethical behavior and illegal practices. That type of failure may end one's professional career.

CLOSING THOUGHT: YOU ARE NOW AN EVEN MORE CAPABLE PERSON

Even if you have, for the time being, "failed" as a sole proprietor, your experience will likely have been far better than the alternative of continuing what you were doing. That would probably have been more of the same as you moved monotonously along the ever-flattening portion of the learning curve. You at least tried to remedy an unsatisfactory employee situation. You had the courage to take a chance. Temporary failure is better than lasting regret. As someone anonymously said: "The opposite of taking risks, is having regrets."

Furthermore, you will never be the same, no matter what you do. You will be different and probably be better as a result of your free lance experience. Regardless of whether you try again as a sole proprietor or return to employee status, you will have grown in many ways. For example, you will have developed additional skills, acquired valuable knowledge, created new visions, and made influential contacts. As stated by Oliver Wendell Holmes:

Man's mind, once stretched by a new idea, never regains its original dimensions.

Finally, because you are a different and more capable person, other opportunities will appear and you will have the insight to see them. In the near future, those opportunities will be in an employee role. In the distant future, they may be elsewhere. Be sure to look for them.

When one door closes, another one opens, but we often look so long and so regretfully upon the closed one that we do not see which one has opened. (Alexander Graham Bell)

REVIEW

In summary, reflect on the main points in this chapter "What if You Fail?" Success as a sole proprietor, individual practitioner or free lance entails risking failure. Don't give up too soon but recognize that you may have to call it quits. If you decide to re-enter the employment market, your "failure" in going out on your own is likely to be viewed as an asset. The asset argument assumes you did not fail because of unethical practices, errors and omissions, or failing to deliver. Even if you fail flying solo, you are now an even more capable person.

Consider this closing thought offered by Henry Ford:

Failure is only the opportunity to begin again more intelligently.

References

Adams, S. 1996. *The Dilbert Principle*, Harper Business, New York, NY.

Allen, C. L. 1988. "The Angry Retort Against Tort Law," *Insight*, October 31.

Allen, J. (no date). *As a Man Thinketh*, Peter Pauper Press.

American Consulting Engineers Council. 1999. "Firms Accept More Work," *American Consulting Engineer*, March/April.

American Society of Civil Engineers. 1999. "Code of Ethics," *Official Register – 1999*, New York, NY, pp. 10-13.

American Society of Civil Engineers. 1990. *Quality in the Constructed Project - A Guideline for Owners, Designers and Constructors* - Volume I.

Andrews, A. S. and W. P. Ruzzo. 1988. "Avoiding Litigation," *Journal of Management in Engineering - ASCE*, Vol. 4, No. 1, January, pp. 8-15.

Ashton, A. and R. Ashton. 1999. "Long-Distance Relationships," *Home Office Computing*, Vol. 17, No. 7, July, pp. 52-55.

Avila, E. A. 1995. "Demystifying the Local Agency's Process of Consultant Procurement," *Journal of Management in Engineering – ASCE*, Vol. 11, No. 5, September/October, pp. 21-23.

Backman, L. 1993. "Computer-Aided Liability," *Civil Engineering - ASCE*, June, pp. 41-43.

Bakan, L. H. 1985. "The Client Relationship: Effective Marketing Steps," *Journal of Management in Engineering - ASCE,* Vol. 1, No. 1, January, pp. 3-11.

Barker, J. A. 1989. *Discovering the Future: The Business of Paradigms*, ILI Press, St. Paul, MN.

Benun, I. (no date). "133 Tips to Promote Yourself & Your Business," Hoboken, NY.

Benun, I. 1999. *The Art of Self Promotion*, Number 26, Winter/Spring.

Benun, I. 2000. *The Art of Self Promotion*, Number 28, Winter/Spring.

Bergeron, H. E. 1999. "Simple Services, Inc.: A Project Management Case Study," *Journal of Management in Engineering – ASCE,* Vol. 15, No. 1, May/June, pp. 33-42.

Binsacca, R. 2000. "Avoiding Overload," *Civil Engineering - ASCE,* Vol. 70, No. 1, January, pp. 54-55.

Biswas, A. K. 1970. *History of Hydrology*, North Holland Publishing Co., Amsterdam.

Bode, R. 1993. *First You Have to Row a Little Boat*, Warner, New York, NY.

Boldt, L. G. 1993. *Zen and the Art of Making a Living: A Practical Guide to Creative Career Design*, Penguin Books, New York, NY.

Bradley, H. 2000. "Building a Customer Database," *Home Office Computing*, Vol. 18, No. 2, February, pp. 108-109.

Brown, E. C. 1988. "Putting a Lid on Liability," *Civil Engineering - ASCE,* Vol. 58, No. 7, July, pp. 66-67.

Brown, Jr., H. J. 1991. *Life's Little Instruction Book*, Rutledge Hill Press, Nashville, TN.

Clough, R. H. 1986. *Construction Contracting*, Fifth Edition, John Wiley & Sons, New York, NY.

Competitive Advantage Inc. 1988. "The Competitive Advantage," Sample Issue.

Covey, S. R. 1990. *The 7 Habits of Highly Effective People*, Simon & Schuster, New York, NY.

Crosby, P. B. 1979. *Quality is Free: The Art of Making Quality Certain*, Mentor Books.

Cypert, S. A. 1993. *The Success Breakthrough*, Avon Books, New York, NY.

Davis, B. H. 1987/1988. "How and Why to Hire a Consultant," *The Whole Non-Profit Catalog*, Winter, pp. 7-9.

Davis, K. and W. B. Ledbetter. 1988. "What Is It and How Do You Get It?," Forum, *Civil Engineering - ASCE*, July.

Davis, R. 2000. "Contract Engineers Build a Temporary Future," *Engineering Times*, Vol. 22, No. 2, February, p. 1.

Davis, R. O. 1986. "Advantages of Standard Contract Forms," *Journal of Management in Engineering - ASCE*, Vol. 2, No. 2, April, pp. 79-90.

Dawson, R. 1995. "Secrets of Power Negotiating," *Success*, September, pp. 57-64.

de Camp, L. S. 1963. *The Ancient Engineers*, Ballantine, New York, NY.

Dehne, G. C. 1991. "How Small Colleges Can Thrive in the '90s," *AGB Reports*, July/August, pp. 6-11.

Devonshire Financial Corporation. 1988. "Sales and Marketing Digest," August.

Dickson, P. 1978/1979. "The Official Rules of Engineering," *New Engineer*, December/January, pp. 56-60.

DPIC Companies. 1988. *Lessons in Professional Liability: A Notebook for Design Professionals*, Monterey, CA.

Dunham, C. W., R. D. Young, and J. T. Bockrath. 1979. *Contracts, Specifications, and Law for Engineers*, Third Edition, McGraw-Hill Book Company, New York, NY.

Dupies, D. A. 1979. "Marketing for Engineering Organizations: Some Experiences," presented at the ASCE National Convention, Boston, MA, April 2-6.

Economist. 1999. "When Companies Connect," June 26, pp. 19-20.

Economist. 1999. "Toiling From Here to There," December 31, p. 22.

Emerson, R. W. 1936. *Essays*, Spencer Press.

Fenske, S. M. and T. E. Fenske. 1989. "Business Planning for New Engineering Consulting Firms," *Journal of Management in Engineering - ASCE*, Vol. 5, No. 1, January, pp. 89-95.

Forbes. 1999. *Forbes ASAP*, A Forbes Supplement, April 5.

Gallant, R. W. 1991. *How to be a Manager*, Lewis Publishers, Chelsea, MI.

Georgia, B. L. 1999. "Are You a Home Office Outlaw?" *Home Office Computing*, Vol. 17, No. 7, July, pp. 86-87.

Gerston, J. 1994. "The Art of Negotiating," *Hemispheres*, September, pp. 43-46.

Groob, J., K. Shockey, L. Watters, and T. Aluise. 1987. "Proven Tips for Marketing Professional Services," *Journal of Management in Engineering - ASCE*, Vol. 3, No. 1, January, pp. 28-37.

Handy, C. 1998. *The Hungry Spirit*, Broadway Books, New York, NY.

Hayden, Jr., W. M. 1987. Quality by Design Newsletter, May, A/E QMA Jacksonville, FL (Quoted in *Journal of Management in Engineering - ASCE,* Vol. 4, No. 4, October 1988, pp. 284-285).

Heightchew, Jr., R. E. 1999. "Selling With Integrity to Develop Your Engineering Practice," *Journal of Management in Engineering – ASCE,* Vol. 15, No. 3, May/June, pp. 47-51.

Hensey, M. D. (Editor). 1987. "The Top 25," in "Management Forum," *Journal of Management in Engineering - ASCE*, Vol. 3, No. 4, October, p. 263.

Hewlett-Packard. 1995. "The Baron Group: Telling Selling Secrets," *Hewlett-Packard Resolution*, Fall, pp. 6-7.

Hill, N. 1960. *Think and Grow Rich*, Fawcett, New York, NY.

Holtz, H. 1987. *Expanding Your Consulting Practice with Seminars*, John Wiley & Sons, Inc., New York, NY.

Huber, P. 1988. "Don't Innovate, It's Dangerous," Forum, *Civil Engineering - ASCE,* April, p. 6.

Huntington, C. G. 1989. “A Craftsman’s Obsession,” Forum, *Civil Engineering - ASCE*, February, p. 6.

Isphording, J. 1990. “Simple Marketing Techniques for the Service Profession,” in “Management Forum,” *Journal of Management in Engineering - ASCE*, Vol. 6, No. 1, January, pp. 12-13.

Kamm, L. J. 1989. *Successful Engineering - A Guide to Achieving Your Goals*, McGraw-Hill, New York, NY.

Kasma, D. R. 1987. “Consultant Selection,” *Journal of Management in Engineering - ASCE*, Vol. 3, No. 4, October, pp. 288-296.

Kotler, P. and K.F.A. Fox. 1985. *Strategic Marketing for Educational Institutions*, Prentice-Hall, Inc., Englewood Cliffs, NJ.

Koltnow, E. and L. S. Dumas. 1990. *Congratulations! You’ve Been Fired*, Fawcett Columbine, New York, NY.

Lancaster, H. 1999. “How To Pick Up Pieces After You’re Fired,” *Herald Tribune*, April 14.

Lancaster, H. 1999. “High-Tech Workers Pay a Price for Accepting Rewards to Stay Put,” *Wall Street Journal*, May 18.

Lantos, P. R. 1998. “Marketing 101: How I Got My Ten Largest Assignments,” *Journal of Management Consulting*, Vol. 10, No. 2, November, pp. 38-39.

Latamore, G. B. 1999. “No Risk, No Reward,” *Today’s Engineer*, Vol. 2, No. 3, Autumn.

Lindeburg, M. R. 1997. *Getting Started as a Consulting Engineer*, Professional Publications, Belmont, CA.

MacLean, W. G. 1982. "Managing Liability: The Insurer's Perspective," *Managing Liability: The Individual's Challenge - The Organization's Challenge - The Manager's Challenge*, Proceedings of a Symposium sponsored by the Engineering Management Division - ASCE, J. R. King, Jr, Editor, Las Vegas, NV, April, pp. 29-39.

Mandino, O. 1968. *The Greatest Salesmen in the World*, Bantam Books, New York, NY.

Martin, J. C. 1993. *The Successful Engineer: Personal and Professional Skills – A Sourcebook*, McGraw-Hill, New York, NY.

McKimmie, K. 2000. "Small Business Bucks: Financing Options for Start-Ups and Expansions," *Indiana Business Magazine*, January, pp. 22-25.

McQuillan, J. A. 1984. "The CE as an Expert Witness," *Consulting Engineer*, January, pp. 48-50.

Miller, D. W. 1987. "Loss Prevention: Safeguards Against Liability," *Journal of Management in Engineering - ASCE*, Vol. 3, No. 2, April, pp. 95-115.

Miller, M. 1974. *Plain Speaking: An Oral Biography of Harry S. Truman*, Berkley Publishing Corporation, New York, NY.

Mishkin, B. and A. E. Schwartz. 1990. "Architect/Engineer Liability for Use of Computer Technology in Designing Projects," Professional Ethics Report—Newsletter of the American Association for the Advancement of Science, Vol. III, No. 2, Spring, pp. 6-7.

Modern Maturity. 2000. "25 Ways to Reinvent Yourself," Vol. 43W, No. 1, January-February, pp. 38-41.

Morton, R. J. 1983. *Engineering Law, Design Liability and Professional Ethics*, Section I-4, "Business Associations," Professional Publications, San Carlos, CA.

National Society of Professional Engineers. 1999. "Survey Reveals Hourly A/E Billing Rates on Increase," *Engineering Times*, November.

National Society of Professional Engineers. 1999. "Professional Engineers in Private Practice Directory of Professional Liability Insurance Carriers," *Engineering Times*, December, pp. 20-22.

Neufeldt, V. (Editor). 1994. *Webster's New World Dictionary of American English*, Third College Edition, Prentice Hall, New York, NY.

Nevins, M. D. and S. A. Stumpf. 1999. "21st – Century Leadership: Redefining Management Education," *Strategy – Management – Competition*, Reprint No. 99305, Booz-Allen & Hamilton, Third Quarter, pp. 41-51.

O'Connor, M. 1999. "Extra! Extra! Read All About It!" *CE News*, December, pp. 40-42.

Olden, R. E. 1991. "Focus on the Business of Professional Design," *Sun/Coast Architect/Builder*, Vol. 56, No. 3, March, pp. 30-31.

Parsons, J. 1999. "Beware of These Six Traps on the Liability Insurance Trail," *American Consulting Engineer*, Vol. 10, No. 5, September/October, pp. 23-25.

Peck, M. S. 1997. *The Road Less Traveled and Beyond: Spiritual Growth in an Age of Anxiety*, Simon & Schuster, New York, NY.

Perlstein, D. 1998. *Solo Success*, Three Rivers Press, New York, NY.

Peters, T. J. and R. H. Waterman, Jr. 1982. *In Search of Excellence*, Harper and Row, New York, NY.

Petroski, H. 1985. *To Engineer is Human: The Role of Failure in Successful Design*, St. Martin's Press, New York, NY.

Pipher, M. 1999. *Another Country: Navigating the Emotional Terrain of Our Elders*, Riverhead Books, New York, NY.

Pirsig, R. M. 1974. *Zen and the Art of Motorcycle Maintenance*, Bantam Books, New York, NY.

Preziosi, D. 1988. "Reviewing Peer Review," *Civil Engineering - ASCE*, November, pp. 46-48.

Rabeler, R. C. 1991. "Maintaining Existing Clients," *Journal of Management In Engineering - ASCE*, Vol. 7, No. 1, January, pp. 21-32.

Roemer, C. 1989. "Business Ownership," *Michiana Executive Journal*, August, pp. 48-52.

Schillaci, W. C. 1995. "A Management Approach to Placing Articles in Engineering Trade Journals," *Journal of Management in Engineering – ASCE*, September/October, pp. 17-20.

Severn, S. R. T., S. C. Gladden and K. S. Nakhjiri. 1994. "Seminars: A Tool for Marketing Professional Services," *Journal of Management in Engineering - ASCE*, Vol. 10, No. 1, January/February, pp. 14-18.

Sheridan, J. H. 1988. "Memos," *Industry Week*, Vol. 237, No. 1, July 4, p. 5.

Smallowitz, H. and D. Molyneux. 1987. "Engineering a Marketing Plan," *Civil Engineering - ASCE*, August, pp. 70-72.

Snyder, J. 1993. *Marketing Strategies for Engineers*, American Society of Civil Engineers, New York, NY.

Stanley, T. J. and W. D. Danko. 1996. *The Millionaire Next Door*, Pocket Books, New York, NY.

Stephens, S. 1993. "Corporations Not Panacea on Personal Liability," *Engineering Times*, November, p. 9.

Stern, G. M. 2000. "Avoid Impulsive Reaction if You're Demoted," *Investor's Business Daily*, May 17.

Stone, D. 1999. "How to Get Paid," *American Consulting Engineer*, September/October, pp. 4-5.

Talbot, D. W. 1998. "Marketing Is Everyone's Job," *Civil Engineering – ASCE*, November, p. 67.

Townsend, R. 1970. *Up the Organization*, Alfred A. Kropf, New York, NY.

Vansant, R. E. 1982. "Liability: Attitudes and Procedures," *Managing Liability: The Individual's Challenge -The Organization's Challenge - The Manager's Challenge*, Proceedings of a Symposium sponsored by the Engineering Management Division - ASCE, J. R. King, Jr, Editor, Las Vegas, NV, April, pp. 23-28.

Vansant, R. E. 1983. "Papering the Job Can Pay Off in the Courtroom," *The Construction Specifier*, September, pp. 14-15.

Wahby, D. 1993. "Managing the A/E Firm in Turbulent Times," in Management Forum, *Journal of Management in Engineering - ASCE*, Vol. 9, No. 2, April, pp. 122-124.

Walesh, S. G. 1993. "Interaction With the Public and Government Officials in Urban Water Planning," presented at Hydropolis - The Role of Water in Urban Planning, Wageningen, The Netherlands, March. Proceedings published in 1995 by Bachhuys Publishers, Leiden, The Netherlands.

Walesh, S. G. 1995. *Engineering Your Future*, Prentice Hall, Englewood Cliffs, NJ.

Walesh, S. G. 1996. "It's Project Management, Stupid!" *Journal of Management in Engineering – ASCE*, Vol. 12, No. 1, January/February, pp. 14-17.

Walesh, S. G. 1997. "Job Security Is An Oxymoron," *Civil Engineering – ASCE*, Vol. 67, No. 2, February, pp. 62-63.

Washington, L. 1999. "Help With Your Home Work," *Money*, February, pp. 163-164.

Zbar, J. D. 2000. "Separate Checks Please: How to Draw the Line Between Business and Personal Finance," *Home Office Computing*, Vol. 18, No. 2, February, pp. 73-76.

Zweig White & Associates. 1999. *The 1999 Fee and Billing Survey of A/E/P and Environmental Consulting Firms.*

Bibliography

Birnberg, H. G., "Communicating the Company's Operating Performance Data," *Journal of Management in Engineering - ASCE*, Vol. 1, No. 1, January, 1985, pp. 12-19. (Discussed by M. D. Hensey in the *Journal*, Vol. 1, No. 3, July 1985, p. 175).

Cori, K. A., "Project Work Plan Development," Presented at the Project Management Institute and Symposium, Atlanta, GA, October, 1989.

Dillon, K., "Questions Would Be Founders Ask," *State of Small Business*, 1998, pp. 57-58.

Fishman, S. (no date). *Wage Slave No More: Law and Taxes For The Self-Employed*, Second Edition, Nolo.com, http://www.nolo.com/Academic/Acad.index.html, Berkeley, CA.

Florman, S. C., *The Civilized Engineer*, St. Martin's Press, New York, NY, 1987.

Fromartz, S. "Taking Charge: Thinking About Reinventing Your Life?" *Modern Maturity*, January-February, 2000, pp. 26-33. (Describes four people who, "…by reinventing their careers, …reinvented their lives.").

Hartley, K. O., "How To Make Project Schedules Really Work For You," *Journal of Management in Engineering - ASCE*, Vol. 9, No. 2, April 1993, pp. 167-173.

Johnson, H. M. and A. Singh, "The Personality of Civil Engineers," *Journal of Management in Engineering – ASCE*, Vol. 14, No. 4, July/August, 1998, pp. 45-56.

Lepatner, B. B. and R. A. Banner, "8 Tips for Avoiding Liability Claims," *American Consulting Engineer*, Second Quarter, 1993, Vol. 4, No. 2, p. 8.

Norris, W. E., "Coping With the Marketplace: A Management Balancing Act," *Journal of Management in Engineering - ASCE*, Vol. 3, No. 3, July, 1987, pp. 194-200.

Oxer, J. P., "The Independent Contractor," Management Digest, *Journal of Management in Engineering – ASCE*, January/February 1999, pp. 18-20.

Vandersluis, C., "Project Management Computer Software Systems," *The Project Manager*, Association for Project Managers, Winter, 1994, pp. 37-39.

Versau, J. A., "Three Strategies for Sure Success: Positioning, Action, People Are Key," *Journal of Management in Engineering - ASCE*, Vol. 2, No. 3, July, 1986, pp. 191-199.

Index

D

E

F

G

To order additional copies of *Flying Solo*, complete the information below.

Ship to: (please print)

Name ______________________________

Address ______________________________

City, State, Zip ______________________________

Day phone ______________________________

_____ copies of *Flying Solo* @ $39.95
(postage included) $ _________

Make check or money order payable to:

Hannah Publishing
3006 Towne Commons Drive
Valparaiso, IN 46385-2979
HannahPublishing@aol.com

- -

To order additional copies of *Flying Solo*, complete the information below.

Ship to: (please print)

Name ______________________________

Address ______________________________

City, State, Zip ______________________________

Day phone ______________________________

_____ copies of *Flying Solo* @ $39.95
(postage included) $ _________

Make check or money order payable to:

Hannah Publishing
3006 Towne Commons Drive
Valparaiso, IN 46385-2979
HannahPublishing@aol.com